A Practical Guide to Finding Treatments That Work for People with Autism

Critical Specialties in Treating Autism and Other Behavioral Challenges

Series Editor
Jonathan Tarbox

A Practical Guide to Finding Treatments That Work for People with Autism

Susan M. Wilczynski
Plassman Family Distinguished Professor of Special
Education and ABA Ball State University
Muncie, IN United States

ACADEMIC PRESS

An imprint of Elsevier
elsevier.com

Academic Press is an imprint of Elsevier
125 London Wall, London EC2Y 5AS, United Kingdom
525 B Street, Suite 1800, San Diego, CA 92101-4495, United States
50 Hampshire Street, 5th Floor, Cambridge, MA 02139, United States
The Boulevard, Langford Lane, Kidlington, Oxford OX5 1GB, United Kingdom

Notices
Knowledge and best practice in this field are constantly changing. As new research and experience broaden our
understanding, changes in research methods or professional practices, may become necessary.

Practitioners and researchers must always rely on their own experience and knowledge in evaluating and using
any information or methods described herein. In using such information or methods they should be mindful of
their own safety and the safety of others, including parties for whom they have a professional responsibility.

To the fullest extent of the law, neither the Publisher nor the authors, contributors, or editors, assume any
liability for any injury and/or damage to persons or property as a matter of products liability, negligence or
otherwise, or from any use or operation of any methods, products, instructions, or ideas contained in the
material herein.

British Library Cataloguing-in-Publication Data
A catalogue record for this book is available from the British Library

Library of Congress Cataloging-in-Publication Data
A catalog record for this book is available from the Library of Congress

ISBN: 978-0-12-809480-8

For Information on all Academic Press publications
visit our website at https://www.elsevier.com

Working together
to grow libraries in
developing countries

www.elsevier.com • www.bookaid.org

Publisher: Nikki Levy
Acquisition Editor: Emily Ekle
Editorial Project Manager: Barbara Makinster
Production Project Manager: Stalin Viswanathan
Designer: Mark Rogers

Typeset by MPS Limited, Chennai, India

CONTENTS

Series Foreword: Critical Specialities in Treating Autism and Other Behavioral Challenges

PURPOSE

The purpose of this series is to provide treatment manuals that address topics of high importance to practitioners working with individuals with autism spectrum disorders (ASD) and other behavioral challenges. This series offers targeted books that focus on particular clinical problems that have not been sufficiently covered in recent books and manuals. This series includes books that directly address clinical specialties that are simultaneously high prevalence (i.e., every practitioner faces these problems at some point) and yet are also commonly known to be a major challenge, for which most clinicians do not possess sufficient specialized training. The authors of individual books in this series are top-tier experts in their respective specialties. The books in this series will help solve the problems that practitioners face by taking the very best in practical knowledge from the leading experts in each specialty and making it readily available in a consumable, practical format. The overall goal of this series is to provide useful information that clinicians can immediately put into practice. The primary audience for this series is professionals who work in treatment and education for individuals with ASD and other behavioral challenges. These professionals include Board Certified Behavior Analysts (BCBAs), Speech and Language Pathologists (SLPs), Licensed Marriage and Family Therapists (LMFTs), school psychologists, and special education teachers. Although not the primary audience for this series, parents and family members of individuals with ASD will find the practical information contained in this series highly useful.

Series Editor
Jonathan Tarbox, PhD, BCBA-D
FirstSteps for Kids
University of Southern California, CA, United States

Dr. Jonathan Tarbox is the Program Director of the Masters of Science in Applied Behavior Analysis program at the University of Southern California, as well as Director of Research and a Regional Clinic Director at FirstSteps for Kids. He is Associate Editor of the journal *Behavior Analysis in Practice* and serves on the editorial boards of five major scientific journals related to autism and behavior analysis. He has published three books on autism treatment and well over 70 peer-reviewed journal articles and chapters in scientific texts. His research focuses on behavioral interventions for teaching complex skills to individuals with autism. He is a frequent presenter at autism and ABA conferences worldwide, and a regular guest on television and radio.

Dr. Susan M. Wilczynski is the Plassman Family Distinguished Professor of Special Education and Applied Behavior Analysis. Before joining the faculty at Ball State University, she served as the Executive Director of the National Autism Center, where she chaired the National Standards Project. The National Standards was the largest comprehensive systematic review of the autism treatment literature of its time. Dr. Wilczynski developed the first center-based treatment program in the state of Nebraska while on faculty at the University of Nebraska Medical Center. As an assistant professor at the University of Southern Mississippi, she supervised the first psychology lab run by a woman in the Psychology department. Dr. Wilczynski has edited multiple books and manuals on evidence-based practice and autism. Most recently, she has published articles related to evidence-based practice and diversity as well as evidence-based practice in non-traditional settings. Dr. Wilczynski has published scholarly works in the *Journal of Applied Behavior Analysis, Behavior Modification, Focus on Autism and Other Developmental Disabilities, Educating and Treating Children*, and *Psychology in the Schools*. She currently serves as on the Practice Board for the Association for Behavior Analysis International. Dr. Wilczynski is a licensed psychologist and a board certified behavior analyst.

ACKNOWLEDGMENTS

I would like to thank a group of scholars who have significantly shaped my thinking about evidence-based practice. I have collaborated with Ronnie Detrich, Timothy Slocum, Trina Spencer, Teri Lewis, and Katie Wolfe on the topic of evidence-based practice and applied behavior analysis. A great deal of this guide was inspired by discussions I have held with them. I would also like to thank Tristram Smith, a leading autism researcher who has also published on the topic of evidence-based practice and ABA. Were it not for his initial publication on this topic, I would not have spent the amount of time necessary to ponder the challenges faced by practitioners as they make decisions to select, retain, adapt, or reject treatments. I would like to thank Mary Ann Wilczynski, my mother, who is my constant cheerleader. I also offer my eternal thanks to Jeff Oresik, my husband, who has given me his unwavering support for more than two decades. My professional and personal adventures would not have allowed me to develop the perspective-taking skills needed to fully explore the topic of evidence-based practice without him.

Evidence-Based Practice: A Brief Overview

As used in this practitioner's guide, the term evidence-based practice (EBP) reflects a practitioner's use of professional judgment to integrate the best available evidence with all relevant client variables in order to select, retain, adapt, and/or reject a treatment. EBP begins with a practitioner seeking the best possible answer to a practical question (e.g., "Can we reduce John's aggression or increase Jalesa's speech?"). Practitioners of any discipline should use the EBP decision-making model to identify effective treatments that can be accurately implemented to meaningfully improve the life of clients. The factors that should enter into this decision-making process remain constant across disciplines. However a special focus on the EBP of applied behavior analysis (ABA) is sometimes made in this guide for two reasons. First, EBP has been introduced to the field of ABA in the last few years. As such, this group of practitioners needs a guide that draws on their ethical guidelines and literature extensively. Second, ABA focuses on changing human behavior. All disciplines require their patients, clients, consumers, or students to change their behavior. For example, all practitioners seek to increase adherence to treatment protocols to improve outcomes for clients (the term client will be used through the remainder of the book). Helping practitioners from all disciplines to understand more about how to produce behavior change should help them meet their own discipline's goals.

This manual shows evidence-based practitioners how to collect all relevant evidence and additional information necessary to fully actualize the EBP decision-making model. The manual is broken into five sections: I. A brief overview; II. Best available evidence; III. Client variables; IV. professional judgment and: V. Conclusions and examples.

Before turning to the decision-making model for EBP, it is important to understand the alternative use of the term "evidence-based practice." There are some professionals in every discipline who use this term to describe treatments that have been systematically evaluated and deemed "effective." Using the term "EBP" in this way is ill fated for three reasons. First, practitioners using the term in this way may believe that randomly selecting a treatment from a list of "approved" treatments will consistently lead to favorable outcomes. They are less likely to use their professional judgment to evaluate both the evidence supporting treatments and the contextual fit (Albin, Lucyshyn, Horner, & Flannery, 1996) based on a range of client variables (e.g., client repertoire, preference, supporting environment, resource constraint, etc.). When favorable outcomes are not forthcoming, a host of negative outcomes may ensue (e.g., the client does not improve, the practitioner may be blamed and terminated, the practitioner may blame the people responsible for implementing the treatment, etc.). Second, practitioners who view a practice as "evidence-based" simply because it appears on a list of systematically evaluated treatments may make weak decisions that will result in poor client outcomes. For example, they could begin implementing interventions without performing the assessments (e.g., functional analysis) that are necessary to identifying treatments that work. Third, using the same term in more than one way leads to poor communication. That is, using the same term in reference to both a procedure and a process is confusing. Instead of using the term "evidence-based" to describe treatments that have been systematically evaluated and deemed "effective," the term "empirically supported treatments" (ESTs) should be used (Drisko & Grady, 2015). However, practitioners should still be cautious when adopting any ESTs without adequate assessment. Before proceeding to Section II, Best Available Evidence, the reader is encouraged to copy the "Evidence-Based Practice Guide" in Appendix A. By reflecting on each component of the decision-making model, as it is reviewed in the guide, practitioners are more likely to see the utility of using this checklist in practice.

Best Available Evidence

Systematic reviews are the most common source of evidence that practitioners using the process of evidence-based practice (EBP) rely on to select, retain, adapt, or reject treatments. However, systematic reviews may not always be available or may not relate sufficiently to the client's current situation to be useful. As a result, other sources of evidence may be useful. For example, practitioners have relied on narrative reviews of the scientific literature for decades. More recently, practice guidelines (i.e., a cross-over between systematic and narrative reviews) have been a highly useful source of information for the evidence-based practitioner. When these sources of evidence are used, they should be supplemented by evidence about the scientific explanations of human behavior (i.e., principles). Evidence that is directly tied to the client will also prove invaluable when using the EBP decision-making model. Client history as well as any current client data may have a significant impact on determining which treatment is best. This section describes each of these sources of evidence, including the strengths and limitations of each method. Evidence-based practitioners can determine how credible the evidence supporting a treatment is and then prioritize (or de-prioritize) different treatments when multiple options are available.

Before proceeding to the description of each source of evidence, practitioners should know how to access evidence regarding systematic reviews and narrative reviews. The most recent systematic and narrative reviews are typically found by reading scientific journals. To identify these articles, evidence-based practitioners must access search engines. Evidence-based practitioners are encouraged to take advantage of university libraries if they maintain an affiliation with a university. Fortunately, there are free search engines that can be used to access relevant systematic reviews if university search engines are not available. For example, Google Scholar is a free search engine that accesses academic journals across a wide range of disciplines. For medical systematic reviews, evidence-based practitioners may choose to use PubMed, available at the following website: http://www.ncbi.nlm.nih.gov/pubmed/. Furthermore, ScienceDirect makes many reviews available by entering keywords such as "systematic review" and "autism." ScienceDirect can be accessed at: http://www.sciencedirect.com/. In addition to using search engines, it can prove highly useful to use clearinghouses that are designed for this purpose. A few examples follow:

- Cochrane Collaboration: http://www.cochrane.org/about-us
- Campbell Collaboration: http://www.campbellcollaboration.org/
- What Works Clearinghouse: http://ies.ed.gov/ncee/wwc/
- National Autism Center: http://www.nationalautismcenter.org/
- National Professional Development Center on Autism Spectrum Disorders: http://autismpdc.fpg.unc.edu/

CHAPTER 1

Systematic Review

Evidence-based practitioners rely on the strongest and most relevant evidence available. A systematic review is the best source of information about treatment effectiveness because it produces the most credible and comprehensive analysis possible (Slocum, Detrich, & Spencer, 2012). Systematic reviews are the least biased source of evidence because: (1) research is identified in a thorough, analytic, and standardized manner, (2) clear procedures are developed for selecting/weighing evidence, (3) the process is transparent and can be replicated, and (4) the objectivity of the process minimizes arbitrary and idiosyncratic decisions because personal decisions are removed from the process (Slocum et al., 2012).

Systematic reviews require a careful analysis of the quality, quantity, and consistency of research findings (Moher, Liberati, Tetzlaff, Altman, & The PRISMA Group, 2009; Slocum et al., 2012). The process of initiating a systematic review typically begins with a team of experts who are motivated to answer one of two types of questions. The experts may ask:

1. "Is a given treatment effective (The term "efficacious" is often used to describe treatments that are effective under research conditions and "effective" is used for treatments that work in real-world settings. In this practitioner's guide, the term "effective" is used to describe both type of treatments that work.)?" (Method #1). In this case the experts examine the evidence of *all populations* with respect to a single treatment (e.g., functional communication training (FCT) or picture schedules).
2. "Are there any effective treatments for a given population (e.g., Autism Spectrum Disorder)?" (Method #2). In this case the experts examine the evidence regarding *all* treatments that have been studied for the population.

Neither approach to systematic reviews is superior; however, the two questions provide different answers. Evidence-based practitioners

A Practical Guide to Finding Treatments That Work for People with Autism.
DOI: http://dx.doi.org/10.1016/B978-0-12-809480-8.00001-7

must understand the difference between these methods so that they know how to use the evidence in the EBP decision-making process. Method #1 will be most useful if a practitioner's goal is to identify the totality of evidence supporting a given treatment. Systematic reviews using Method #1 include every study that has been conducted with diverse populations (e.g., young and old people, individuals with disabilities and those who have no diagnoses, studies completed in schools, homes, hospitals, and communities, etc.). The advantage of a Method #1 systematic review is that practitioners can gain an understanding of *all* of the evidence that is available for *a given* treatment. Because these systematic reviews collect more evidence, it will be easier to determine if the treatment "works." The question remains, "works" for what purpose. When Method #1 systematic reviews are used, evidence-based practitioners must do a lot of work to answer the question, "Is there enough evidence to show this treatment works for a client *like mine*?" To make this determination, evidence-based practitioners will need to ask a series of questions like, "Is there enough evidence that the treatment works for individuals with ASD who: (1) are the same particular age or developmental level as my client?, (2) need to increase/decrease a specific behavior (e.g., adaptive skills, problem behaviors)?, (3) who are in a specific setting?, etc." Evidence-based practitioners often need more specificity than a Method #1 systematic review provides if they hope to answer the practical question that initiated the search for evidence.

When the experts complete a systematic review on all treatments for a specific population (i.e., Method #2), many of these questions are likely to be answered. But evidence-based practitioners still need to examine the data carefully. For example, some treatments are described as "experimental" or having "emerging" evidence in these reviews. That is, the treatment has some evidence of effectiveness, but there is not yet enough evidence to show it works with the population of interest. How do evidence-based practitioners use a Method #2 review that determines a treatment has only emerging evidence, but a Method #1 review shows the treatment is effective when research involving a broader population is evaluated. FCT serves as an excellent example. According to the National Standards Project 2.0 (NSP; National Autism Center (NAC), 2015), FCT has only emerging evidence for individuals with ASD. However, a much broader base of evidence for FCT exists for the disability community in general.

The evidence-based practitioner must use professional judgment to evaluate the usefulness of all sources of information as they apply for the client that is currently being served.

Evidence-based practitioners ask additional questions even when a treatment is identified as effective. Even when the research included in the systematic review involves individuals with ASD, they might be at different age or at a different developmental level than the target client. The setting or the person implementing the treatment might be different. The identified treatment may have worked with participants who are similar to a given client, but the behavior targeted in the research is different than the behavior targeted for the current client. Evidence-based practitioners examine the treatments closely to understand the applicability of research at this level.

When picking the ideal treatment, evidence-based practitioners first identify treatments that have the best available evidence for a given client. The best evidence may come from:

- a systematic review for individuals with ASD that has data broken down based on relevant features (e.g., age, target behavior, etc.);
- an examination of the articles that are included in the systematic review to determine how different the research participants and research setting are from our client's situation;
- a systematic review for individuals with ASD that has been supplemented by a systematic review that includes additional populations.

Evidence-based practitioners make decisions about how best to use all forms of evidence by using their professional judgment (see Section III: Target, Stakeholder, and Leader Clients).

THE PROCESS OF CONDUCTING A SYSTEMATIC REVIEW

To be critical consumers of systematic reviews, evidence-based practitioners need to understand how experts evaluate the strength of the evidence supporting a treatment (Slocum et al., 2012). Systematic reviews consistently focus on the quality, quantity, and consistency of research outcomes. However the criteria scholars use to determine the quality, quantity, and consistency varies considerably across systematic reviews. By understanding criteria used in systematic reviews, evidence-based practitioners can critically evaluate whether or not they find a systematic review credible.

Quality

Experts evaluate the quality of a study because they know that not all published studies provide strong evidence. Quality of studies is based on the research design, dependent variable, and treatment fidelity (i.e., the extent to which a treatment has been accurately implemented). Many studies also include an evaluation of participant ascertainment (i.e., the quality of the methods used to determine the participant's diagnosis/diagnoses) and generalization (i.e., the extent to which the effects of treatment spread to other relevant situations or are maintained over time). Table 1.1 defines these features and identifies common variables that experts use to determine the quality of each study examined in a systematic review. Some systematic reviews also examine social validity (i.e., the extent to which the end users describe a treatment as fair, appropriate and reasonable in a given case; Wolf, 1978). See Section III, Target, Stakeholder, and Leader Clients, for discussion of social validity.

The evidence-based practitioner who critically evaluates systematic reviews should also know that different groups of experts set different inclusion criteria for systematic reviews. Some experts only evaluate randomized controlled trials (RCT) because they view these studies to be of the highest quality. When experts only review studies that reach a very high standard, the majority of published studies are not included in the systematic review. A Cochrane report by Oono, Honey, and McConachie (2013) on parent-mediated early interventions for children with ASD is an example of this type of systematic review. Although it provides highly useful information about this intervention, it ignores the majority of studies conducted in this area. Other systematic reviews include all studies on a given topic/population, irrespective of the quality of the study. This more comprehensive review can inform practitioners when limited or no evidence supports a given treatment. There is no universal inclusion criterion that is better; however, EBP must understand the differences when determining how the results can be applied for the client they are serving.

Increasingly, systematic reviews include studies using single-subject research design (SSRD), but they are often given less credence

Table 1.1 Criteria Commonly Used to Assess Quality of Research Studies

	Research Design	Dependent Variable	Treatment Fidelity	Participant Ascertainment	Generalization
Definition	The method used to determine if the independent variable is functionally related to the dependent variable	The instrument(s) used to measure change	The extent to which an intervention was implemented the way it was designed	The accuracy of the diagnosis for research participants	The continued effectiveness of a treatment after the passage of time and/or that it is effective under conditions that are different than originally studied
Variables commonly evaluated	*Group Research Design* • Randomization • Number of groups • Number of participants • Attrition *Single-subject research design* • Number of comparisons • Number of data points per condition • Number of Participants • Attrition	*Checklists, Tests, etc.* • Type of measurement • Standardization • Psychometric support • Independence of evaluators • Evaluators blind to treatment condition *Observation* • Data type: Continuous/ discontinuous • Interobserver agreement or kappa values • Percentage of session observed • Number of conditions in which behavior was observed	• Treatment fidelity • Volume of treatment fidelity data collected • Interobserver agreement on treatment fidelity	• Qualifications of professional making diagnosis • Independence/blind to condition for evaluators confirming diagnosis for research purpose • Current DSM or ICD criteria met	• Objective data • Sources of data: maintenance, generalization across setting, materials, people

(Moeller, Dattilo, & Rusch, 2015). That is, SSRD are often seen as less credible sources of evidence, but this is not universally the case. For example, the NSP 2.0 (National Autism Center, 2015) is a large-scale systematic review of the ASD literature that considers evidence from SSRD studies to provide strong evidence. Evidence-based practitioners of ABA should particularly rely on systematic reviews that incorporate SSRD because SSRD is the scientific foundation for ABA. However, it is equally important to acknowledge that not all studies using SSRD provide strong evidence. Finally, it is important to understand that all research designs (including RCT and SSRD) are imperfect. That is, it is possible to draw the wrong conclusion because of the limitations of any research design.

Quantity

A single study is not enough to determine if a treatment is effective, even if it is of very high quality. There is a chance a study has produced spurious findings (i.e., outcomes that appear valid but are not). Replication or extension (i.e., conducting a study similar to one already published) of existing literature is a cornerstone of the scientific process. It is only when a treatment effect has been reproduced that the results are considered credible.

Experts establish a criterion regarding the number of studies needed to determine whether or not a treatment is effective prior to completing a systematic review. The type of research design (group vs SSRD) may influence the number of studies required. Those systematic reviews that include SSRD require a larger number of studies to determine that a treatment is effective. For example, the Evidence-Based Practices for Children, Youth and Young Adults with Autism Spectrum Disorders Report (Wong et al., 2015) completed by the National Professional Development Center for Autism Spectrum Disorders uses the decision-making framework offered by Horner et al. (2005). That is, they selected a criterion of at least five studies that have been conducted by at least three independent researchers and at least 20 participants have been included in the research when the research relies on SSRD.

Treatment Categorization and Consistency

In addition to quality and quantity, consistency of outcomes helps determine whether or not a treatment is identified as effective. In some systematic reviews the criteria for identifying consistency are identified.

For example, the NSP 2.0 (National Autism Center, 2015) states that a study reporting conflicting data must (1) be better controlled to be meaningful and (2) clearly show that the treatment was ineffective or had adverse treatment effects to alter the rating of a treatment. If a treatment works in some well-controlled studies but does not work in others, the evidence-based practitioner must use caution before considering the treatment. Furthermore, systematic reviews should include information about harm (e.g., side effects) so that informed treatment selection decisions are made (Khan, Kunz, Kleijnan, & Antes, 2003).

After the quality and quantity of all studies have been evaluated, the outcomes must be combined to determine consistency of outcomes. Studies using the same treatment are put into a single category (e.g., Treatment X). This process is more challenging than it appears at first glance because (1) different studies use the same name to describe treatments that are procedurally very different; (2) different studies use different names to describe treatments that are procedurally very similar, and (3) the question, "How 'pure' does a treatment have to be (e.g., what if it is combined with another treatment)?" must be answered. Determining the meaningful unit for a "treatment" with systematic designs is also very challenging and fraught with controversy (Wilczynski, 2012) and experts in the field of EBP do not sufficiently address this issue at this point in time. Categories can be very small (e.g., time-out) or very large (e.g., behavioral interventions). When evidence-based practitioners do not see the name of the treatment they are interested in using in a systematic review, they should determine if it has been placed into a larger category (e.g., time-out might be in behavioral interventions).

Determining Treatment Effectiveness

Once categories of treatments are formed and data on quality and quantity have been calculated, the results are compared against a criterion representing the level of effectiveness (e.g., two or more well-controlled RCT or five single-subject research design studies). When the criterion is met, a treatment is deemed effective. When the criterion is not met, it might be described as experimental or as having no evidence. Sometimes, a meta-analysis is used to establish the criteria for effectiveness. One challenge with using meta-analysis is that treatments should be very similar when combined to produce meaningful interpretation (Leucht, Kissling, & Davis, 2009). Depending on the size of the treatment category, this might not be feasible. On the other hand, meta-analyses can be extremely helpful when conflicting results are reported. Unfortunately, many studies do not include information that is needed to run a meta-analysis, so the results can be based on a smaller number of studies than have actually been conducted.

All of the decisions described in this section can influence the likelihood a treatment will be called "effective." When more than one systematic review is conducted with a given population, somewhat different results sometimes emerge. Fortunately, many comprehensive systematic reviews have produced very similar outcomes (e.g., NSP 2.0, Wong et al., 2015). However, evidence-based practitioners can look at the method for completing the systematic review and determine which outcomes they find to be most relevant for their clients.

CHAPTER 2

Other Sources of Evidence

There are a number of reasons systematic reviews might not be ideal. First, a relevant systematic review may not have been conducted. Second, the available systematic reviews might not be relevant to the practical question that the evidence-based practitioner is addressing (Slocum, Detrich, & Spencer, 2012). Third, systematic reviews might not be credible because they have become outdated. Fourth, systematic reviews are not perfect sources of evidence and can be susceptible to bias. Two sources of bias are relevant for even the best systematic reviews (Moher, Liberati, Tetzlaff, Altman, & The PRISMA Group, 2009):

1. publication bias (i.e., selective reporting of completed studies because studies showing a treatment that does not work are less likely to be published). For example, most researchers have conducted studies in which a treatment did not work. The researchers put those studies aside because they know a journal will not publish studies on noneffective treatments. To keep their jobs or be competitive for grants, they need to be publishing regularly. As a result, they focus their energy on the next study that is likely to produce positive outcomes.
2. outcome reporting bias (i.e., researchers selectively report positive findings). For example, a researcher may have conducted a study of a treatment that was expected to increase social skills and decrease problem behavior. The treatment effectively decreased problem behavior but did not increase social skills. The researcher submits a study for publication that only includes information about decreasing problem behaviors and does not discuss social skills at all.

Recognizing that systematic reviews provide imperfect evidence encourages the evidence-based practitioner to explore other sources of relevant evidence when needed. Useful alternative sources of evidence include: narrative reviews, evidence-based practice guidelines, scientific principles of behavior, client history, and current client data.

A Practical Guide to Finding Treatments That Work for People with Autism.
DOI: http://dx.doi.org/10.1016/B978-0-12-809480-8.00002-9

NARRATIVE REVIEWS

Narrative reviews include consensus and critical reviews. When a group of scholars create a consensus review (also known as a best practice panel), they draw from their expertise and evaluation of the scientific literature. These experts have been asked to lend their expertise to the review because they are very familiar with the evidence and have been regular contributors to the literature. The greatest weakness of a consensus review results from the potential for bias entering into the final conclusions. Bias may result from the selection process that initiates a review. That is, there is little transparency about how editors or funding agencies select the experts to complete reviews. Editors (of a book, journal, or other document) or funders may include experts who confirm their biases and exclude experts who offer disconfirmatory perspectives (Slocum et al., 2012). The expert may also introduce bias by placing inordinate weight on a single research article or completely ignore another. This form of bias is typically unintentional; however, human beings inadvertently allow bias to influence their conclusions. Group-based bias can also influence the reported outcomes of consensus reviews. For example, when a highly prestigious member of an expert panel states his or her opinion, others may agree without applying due diligence. This source of bias is less likely to occur when experts hold diverse views about the literature. Unfortunately, it is also more difficult to achieve consensus when a larger, more diverse group of experts write a review (Wilczynski, 2012).

A critical review is similar to a consensus review, but it is completed by a single researcher or a group of researchers who have not been invited to discuss their views based on their expertise. These reviews are prone to the same sources of bias as consensus reviews. Despite these limitations, consensus and critical reviews were the primary source of evidence that could guide practitioners until recently. They may still prove very useful, particularly when a systematic review closely matching the characteristics of a given case is not available. Evidence-based practitioners should recognize that a consensus or critical review of the literature may reflect a better fit with the specifics of a given case. For example, a critical review could match the setting, diagnosis for participant, target behavior, etc., in every way—and better than the parameters used to conduct the only available systematic review.

PRACTICE GUIDELINES

Practice guidelines are a crossover between systematic reviews and consensus reviews. They typically begin with a systematic review but then recognize that systematic reviews often leave important questions unanswered. For example, the strength of evidence for treatments that are reviewed may be weak, resulting in virtually no recommendations for practitioners. The experts make broad recommendations based on their expertise while recognizing that the evidence supporting the recommendations is not sufficient. Practice guidelines may also outline resources that are required for accurate implementation, treatment fidelity checklists, and methods for adapting treatments to improve contextual fit (i.e., altering the treatment so it better matches the client characteristics and supporting environment). Although practice guidelines can be very useful, evidence-based practitioners should still use extreme caution when using them. Evidence-based practitioners need to carefully examine which recommendations are based on scientific evidence and which are based on expert opinion. Nonscientific recommendations may be very helpful and should not be ignored; however, they should be used only when alternatives based on evidence are not available. Furthermore, client data will need to be collected very frequently so that the decision to discard or adapt a treatment will occur very quickly when weak empirical support has been presented. Lastly, although these practice guidelines are subject to the same biases as narrative reviews (Slocum et al., 2012) they are still extremely useful to evidence-based practitioners who are careful consumers of these documents.

PRINCIPLES

The scientific principles that explain human behavior also serve as an important source of evidence when selecting treatments. Treatments should be conceptually consistent with scientific explanations of human behavior, so evidence-based practitioners can use the key principles of ABA when they select from an array of treatment options. Consider the following ABA principles:

- There is a functional relationship between behavior and one or more controlling variables in the environment
- Reinforcement (both positive and negative) strengthens behavior

- Punishment weakens behavior
- Removal of reinforcement (extinction) weakens behavior
- Stimuli may occasion responding or discontinuation of responding.

These principles are derived from studies conducted across decades, scientists, populations of interests, and environmental conditions. Principles can serve as a useful source of evidence because they have been supported by research. However, these principles have not been submitted to a systematic review, so the most rigorous process for examining intervention effectiveness has not been imposed. This does not need to present a tremendous problem for the evidence-based practitioner of ABA because treatments that are selected should be conceptually consistent with these principles. Principles should complement other approaches to gathering evidence—not replace them (Slocum et al., 2012).

Evidence-based practitioners often create treatments that include multiple components that are derived from these key principles. Multicomponent treatments have typically not been submitted to a systematic review because there are not enough studies that contain those same elements to warrant a review. For example, a multicomponent treatment for spinning in circles might include functional communication training, extinction, response interruption with redirection, and environmental enrichment. Each of these components is derived from scientific explanations of human behavior. However the unique combination of these treatment components has not been submitted to a systematic review. When clear evidence is not available from other sources of evidence, evidence-based practitioners should still rely on behavioral principles when making decisions to select, retain, adapt, or reject a treatment (Slocum et al., 2014).

Interventions do not always use the exact methods described in studies because they are adapted for the current client or circumstances (Slocum et al., 2012). Principles can help evidence-based practitioners make these adaptations. However, they should be cautious when adapting treatments. The evidence-based practitioner should ask, "Is the treatment we adapted so different from the treatment protocol that was used in research that it is no longer empirically supported?" This question should be asked even when the adaptations are consistent with the scientific principles that explain behavior. Evidence-based practitioners ideally use treatment protocols that closely resemble those used in well-controlled research (i.e., identified as effective in a systematic review) and are based on the scientific principles that explain human behavior. See Chapter 12, Determining the Next Step, for additional recommendations on how to do this.

CLIENT HISTORY

Evidence-based practitioners look at client history to assess the outcomes when specific treatments have been attempted previously. Evidence from a systematic review or other sources of evidence can be supplemented with direct evidence that a treatment is effective with the target client. However, evidence-based practitioners are still critical when evaluating these data because there are a number of reasons the previous results may not reflect whether or not the treatment will be effective now.

Confounding Explanations

If a treatment has worked for a client in the past, it should be given a high priority when selected from an array of treatment options. This prioritization should be taken very seriously when there is evidence that the improvement was due to the treatment. But evidence-based practitioners recognize that the behavior change observed in the past may have been due to some other relevant variable. This can be ruled out by using SSRD in practice (e.g., ABAB, multiple baseline, or multielement design, etc.). In most settings:

1. A problem is identified (behavior needs to decrease or skills need to increase).
2. An assessment leads to intervention (although this step is too often skipped).
3. An intervention is put into place.
4. Outcomes are determined: If the client improves, the treatment is faded and eventually stopped. If the client does not improve, an alternative intervention is attempted.

Although this approach is practical, it does not provide compelling data because there might be an alternate explanation. If the treatment "worked," it could be because some other important factor changed (e.g., a treatment was implemented in another setting). If the treatment did not work, it could be because the intervention was not implemented long enough (i.e., everyone gave up on the treatment too soon).

Treatment Fidelity

"If the treatment was not effective in the past, is there evidence the treatment was implemented accurately?" Treatments are often attempted and rejected without any evidence it was accurately implemented, when it is possible that the desired behavior change did not occur because the treatment was not delivered properly. Without treatment fidelity data (i.e., the extent to which an intervention is accurately implemented), there is no compelling reason to reject a treatment as ineffective. Imagine going to the doctor with a migraine. The doctor says you are going to be given some migraine medication. The nurse gives you a baby aspirin and a few hours later you still have your migraine. The doctor responds, "Well, I guess that migraine medication does not work!" Exasperated, you find another doctor. "Would you tell the next doctor that you have tried migraine medication in the past and it did not work?" Of course not! You would not reject the migraine medication as a good option simply because you took a pill that held minor resemblance to it. Unfortunately, when treating individuals with ASD, this type of decision-making happens too often. That is, a behavioral or educational treatment is rejected as "ineffective" even though it has never really been implemented. Evidence-based practitioners do not reject treatments described as "ineffective" based on client history unless treatment fidelity data show that the intervention was accurately implemented. Additional information about treatment fidelity can be found in Chapter 8, Treatment Feasibility and Social Validity.

Different Environmental Conditions

A variety of environmental conditions can support or undermine treatment effectiveness. Even when a treatment was not effective in the past and it was accurately implemented, the evidence-based practitioner may consider it appropriate if the environmental conditions are substantially different. For example, a teacher might have attempted a treatment in the past with a student on the autism spectrum. The treatment was not successful because the student could not attend to relevant stimuli during the intervention due to distracting elements in the classroom (e.g., there were several students who broke class rules when the teacher was working individually with a student). The evidence-based practitioner discusses this treatment option with the resource teacher, who will be working individually with the same student. This treatment might be deemed preferable to other options under the new circumstances. As will be seen throughout this guide, practitioners must consider multiple forms of evidence and weigh a wide range of client and contextual variables when decisions are made to initially select, retain, adapt, or reject a given treatment.

Current Client Data

Evidence-based practitioners are data-driven and must therefore use current data as an invaluable source of evidence. Consider the case of Christopher, an 8-year-old boy who consistently disrupts others in his classroom. During the information-gathering phase, the evidence-based practitioner begins a functional behavioral assessment to generate a hypothesis about the function of behavior. Based on the scatterplot, an interview with Christopher's teacher, and A-B-C data, the function of the behavior appears to be automatic reinforcement. Clearly the data in the current case can be used in conjunction with other sources of information about evidence (e.g., systematic reviews) to select an effective function-based intervention. Any other source of evidence that helps identify the "best" treatment option should be given consideration and weighed based on how compelling this source of evidence may be.

Target, Stakeholder, and Leader Client Variables, Values, and Preferences

The target client is the direct recipient of an intervention. In addition to client history and current data, evidence-based practitioners consider the target client's health, the skills in their client's repertoire, their preferences, and the social validity of the intervention when selecting treatments.

Stakeholder clients usually play a fundamental role in selecting and implementing interventions that are designed to increase appropriate behaviors/developmental skills or decrease problem behaviors for individuals with ASD. Stakeholder clients have regular, direct contact with the target client (e.g., daycare worker, teacher, direct service provider, or parents of the individual with ASD). Evidence-based practitioners should assess the social validity of treatments (e.g., acceptability, family's quality of life, etc.) as well as the feasibility of each treatment option before selecting treatments. Feasibility involves assessing the resources required to implement interventions and the environmental supports that enhance or undermine the likelihood of treatment fidelity. Treatment fidelity is an indicator of feasibility because if a treatment cannot be accurately implemented, the treatment is probably not appropriate given the context. Evidence-based practitioners also evaluate stakeholder clients' views as to whether or not it would be feasible to sustain the intervention.

In many schools or agencies, administrative professionals or thought leaders make systemic decisions about the appropriateness of a given treatment. For example, principals or center directors may wish to increase the school's or agency's capacity to serve a given population (e.g., ASD). In addition to feasibility, these leader clients consider the impact on the entire organization, including their match with cultural norms and the likelihood of producing benefit for other students or clients.

CHAPTER 3

Client Health

According to the Professional and Ethical Compliance Code for Behavior Analysts (BACB, 2014), practitioners should recommend their clients seek "medical consultation if there is any reasonable possibility that a referred behavior is influenced by medical or biological variables." To meet this ethical obligation, evidence-based practitioners become informed about how medications, medical and comorbid conditions, and biological variables can influence behavior. Evidence-based practitioners use this information to influence the treatment selection process.

MEDICATION

Evidence-based practitioners become familiar with medications taken by their target clients and the potential side effects of these medications. The more common side effects of psychotropic medications include headaches, gastrointestinal discomfort/distress, changes in weight (sometimes significant), and sleep disturbances. Any of these common side effects can directly and/or indirectly impact behavior. Less common but serious side effects of psychotropic medications for children are cardiovascular irregularities, suicidal ideation, and hypersensitivity events (Garcia, Logan, & Gonzalez-Heydrich, 2012).

Physicians may prescribe more than one psychotropic treatment simultaneously and some medications are prescribed off label (i.e., in way that is not approved by regulatory bodies such as the FDA; Good & Gelled, 2016). It is important to ask about medication usage both at the onset of treatment and throughout service delivery because medication use may change over time. Physicians may alter the dosage of an existing medication, change the medication, or prescribe additional medications to the target client. When the evidence-based practitioner is unaware of medication usage or changes, problems may be

A Practical Guide to Finding Treatments That Work for People with Autism.
DOI: http://dx.doi.org/10.1016/B978-0-12-809480-8.00003-0

incorrectly attributed to environmental factors. Several undesirable outcomes could result:

- The target behavior improves but the practitioner attributes the improvement to a time- or cost-intensive behavioral intervention. The intervention is continued and valuable resources are unnecessarily expended.
- The target behavior remains the same. The client remains on a medication with potential side effects because the physician does not receive feedback about ineffectiveness.
- The target behavior worsens and a costly functional analysis is conducted to develop a potentially inappropriate intervention (i.e., based on the incorrect function).
- The target client needlessly experiences unpleasant side effects.

By maintaining an ongoing dialog about medications, evidence-based practitioners can encourage caregivers to adhere to a medication schedule or discourage caregivers from altering medication levels independently. In addition, physicians recommend frequent monitoring of children and adolescents who are taking psychotropic medications (Garcia et al., 2012), so evidence-based practitioners can not only make referrals for medical evaluations but also work collaboratively with prescribing physicians regarding behavior change.

MEDICAL AND COMORBID CONDITIONS

Pain

Many medical conditions should impact the treatment decisions evidence-based practitioners make. Pain is often associated with problem behavior among children with ASD and other developmental disabilities (Courtemanche, Black, & Reese, 2016). Many individuals with ASD are not able to effectively communicate about their pain, and careful observation of pain-related behaviors is necessary to understand the relationship between pain and problem behavior. The Non-Communicating Children's Pain Checklist Revised (NCCPC-R; Breau, McGrath, Camfield, & Finley, 2002) has been used to examine the relationship between pain and self-injury, aggression, and stereotypic behaviors. Evidence-based practitioners should make every effort to assess pain, prior to conducting additional analyses (e.g., functional behavioral assessment or functional analyses), particularly among people who are unable to easily communicate about their experiences of pain. Evidence-based practitioners refer any target clients with ASD for medical evaluations if pain could be a factor related to problem behavior.

Restraint

Injuries such as bites, damage to joints, broken bones, or friction burns may result from restraint procedures. Approximately 142 deaths occurred during the 1990s as a result of physical restraint (Council for Children with Behavioral Disorders, 2009) and this is reason enough to avoid using this procedure. However, there are target clients who have medical conditions that make restraint contraindicated. For example, individuals who are obese or have a history of heart conditions are particularly at risk for serious side effects (e.g., deep vein thrombosis and resulting pulmonary embolism; Ishida et al., 2014). Evidence-based practitioners must be aware of all medical conditions that may indicate physical restraint or any other procedure should not be used.

Seizures

A large number of individuals with ASD also have epilepsy (15–30%; van Iterson, De Jong, & Zijlstra, 2015). Epilepsy can be associated with seizure-induced aggression (i.e., aggression associated with frontal lobe seizures; Gedye, 1989). If evidence-based practitioners are not aware that a significant percentage of individuals with ASD have co-occurring epilepsy and that aggressions can be seizure induced, they are likely to invest considerable resources to identify the function of behavior when the seizure is the real source of the aggression. Because petit mal seizures may not be immediately obvious to stakeholder clients (i.e., adults working directly with the client), evidence-based practitioners should be trained to identify potential symptoms of epilepsy.

BIOLOGICAL VARIABLES

Biological variables can serve as motivating operations (i.e., conditions that momentarily alter the effectiveness of reinforcers). For example, hunger can impact any range of behaviors directly (e.g., difficulty paying attention to work) and indirectly (e.g., preferred activities like running around and playing are no longer valuable and do not serve as reinforcers). Similarly, sleep deprivation can influence the capacity to learn (because a target client is less able to attend to relevant details), remember newly acquired information, self-regulate under distress. Further, sleep deprivation can make task demands aversive, even if the client normally tolerates them when not sleep deprived. High rates of problem behavior can occur when a target client is sleep deprived. Many children with ASD experience significant sleep dysfunction (Kennedy & Meyer, 1996) and treatments that should be effective may not produce change. Evidence-based practitioners refer individuals with chronic sleep deprivation to sleep specialists.

Stamina (i.e., physical capacity to sustain effort) is also a biological variable that can serve as a motivating operation. Many individuals with ASD do not receive sufficient opportunities to exercise (Place, 2015) or exercise is given a lower priority than learning to speak, interact with others, and develop academic or work skills. Yet stamina can directly impact progress in each of these domains. Consider a 10-year-old girl with ASD who is not making progress across multiple program goals. Although she performs independently and accurately in the morning, all trials in the afternoon show a decrement in performance. Her capacity to physically perform activities in the afternoon is poorer as a result of a weak core (i.e., holding her body erect in her seat and then reaching for and selecting the correct item from an array is physically challenging). In addition, the value of reinforcers can be diminished if the item involves manipulation (e.g., a toy) or activity. In all cases, biological variables can have both a direct and an indirect impact on behavior by altering the rate of behavior and the value of reinforcers. Decisions to retain, adapt, or reject treatments are dependent on ongoing evaluation of these biological variables.

MENTAL HEALTH

Many individuals with ASD hold co-occurring (comorbid) diagnoses. These comorbid conditions should impact treatment decisions. Attention-deficit hyperactivity disorder (Musser et al., 2014; Russell, Rodgers, Ukoumunne, & Ford, 2014), disruptive behavior disorders (now known as other specified or unspecified disruptive, impulse control, and conduct disorder; De Bruin, Ferdinand, Meester, deNijs, & Verheih, 2007), anxiety disorders, and depression (including suicidal ideation; Hammond & Hoffman, 2014) are the most common comorbid conditions for individuals with ASD. These disorders are often treated with medication, so evidence-based practitioners should be familiar with medication effects and side effects. Evidence-based practitioners need to refer target clients to qualified professionals who can complete comprehensive assessments for comorbid conditions whenever symptoms that are not characteristic of ASD are present. In addition, they use information about comorbidity to interpret behavior. For example, if a socially avoidant behavior is associated with increased levels of anxiety, the intervention would more likely involve progressive relaxation training than if the social avoidance is merely associated with a thin schedule of reinforcement.

Evidence-based practitioners should consider the possibility a comorbid condition exists even when a diagnosis has not been rendered. For example, abuse among individuals with disabilities is pervasive (Wilczynski, Connolly, DuBard, Henderson, & McIntosh, 2015). Behavior analysts, like other practitioners, have the ethical responsibility to use positive procedures before considering aversive techniques (BACB, 2014). However the responsibility to avoid these procedures are even greater when a target client has a history of abuse. Given the limitations in communication that many individuals with ASD have, the evidence-based practitioner may have difficulty learning about an abuse history (Wilczynski et al., 2015), so they should err on the side of avoiding aversive procedures, particularly those that are topographically similar to abuse. Abuse may come at the hands of care providers but also peers (bullying, dating violence). Evidence-based practitioners include information in a client's history regarding bullying when they lead the process of selecting a best treatment. For example, a peer-mediated intervention is likely not appropriate for a client with a history of bullying until the process of supervising and gradually introducing peers in a safe and unthreatening manner is identified. Adequately assessing abuse and bullying should be completed by a professional with significant training in this sensitive area. Evidence-based practitioners should refer to qualified professionals (e.g., psychologists) if any history of abuse is suspected.

Qualified professionals should also assess for a history of substance abuse. Individuals with substance abuse problems avoid confronting their problems and have more reactions that are palliative (e.g., smoking or drinking to distract themselves from problems) and passive (e.g., socially withdraw, ruminate about their problems, think about their inability to solve a problem). Individuals with ASD who abuse substances are no exception, but they are also less likely to express their emotions or have reassuring thoughts about problem resolution (Kronenberg, Goossens, van Busschback, van Achterberg, & van den Brink, 2015). Evidence-based practitioners should refer to a substance abuse specialist if they suspect a target client is abusing alcohol or illegal substances. Individuals with ASD and substance abuse disorders have happier and more productive lives when they have structure, but abuse of substances is associated with a disordered life and poorer initiative (Kronenberg, Slager-Visscher, Goossens, van Den Brink, & van Achterberg, 2014). A team of professionals may be needed to adequately identify the best intervention.

CHAPTER 4

Client Repertoire and Behavioral Cusps

Practitioners typically evaluate client repertoire (i.e., the skills a client has already mastered) to identify new skills that should be targeted for improvement. However, when an array of appropriate treatments are feasible for a given client, understanding the skills that are within the client's repertoire can help evidence-based practitioners identify the best intervention option.

CLIENT REPERTOIRE

Treatments cannot be plucked off a list of empirically supported treatments and be expected to work. There are prerequisite skills that must be mastered in order for a treatment to be effective. For example, video modeling is often identified as an effective treatment for individuals with ASD (National Autism Center, 2015; Wong et al., 2015), but it is only effective if clients have the prerequisite skills in their repertoire. Video modeling involves presenting a visual recording of a skillfully completed task, so that a target client can imitate the task. In order to benefit from video modeling, a target client must be able to (1) remain still enough to (2) attend to all pertinent aspects of the model and stimuli in order to (3) imitate each critical step of the task until ideally, (4) the skill is generalized to all relevant situations (e.g., settings, materials, instructors, etc.). Evidence-based practitioners should assess whether or not a target client possesses these skills prior to selecting video modeling as the intervention of choice. Although additional programming can address generalization of skills, items 1−3 must be in the client's repertoire if video modeling can reasonably be expected to work at all. Even if a skill can be developed through video modeling, the treatment may not be ideal if the client is not able to take the skill and use it in other relevant settings (e.g., home, school, community), with other relevant materials (i.e., similar but nonidentical stimuli that serve the same purpose as the training materials), and in the company of other relevant individuals (e.g., family

A Practical Guide to Finding Treatments That Work for People with Autism.
DOI: http://dx.doi.org/10.1016/B978-0-12-809480-8.00004-2

members, classmates, community members, and/or helpers). Evidence-based practitioners do not select video modeling because they have heard that clients with ASD are "visual learners." Instead, they identify the prerequisite skills needed for treatment effectiveness and then evaluate the degree to which each client possesses these skills prior to treatment selection.

Another example will further this point. Individuals with ASD have qualitative impairments in social-communication skills. As a result, social skills programs are often selected to treat these clients. Like video modeling, social skills programs involve remaining still enough to attend to all pertinent aspects of training. There is the additional demand that the target client attend to these relevant features when other (and potentially distracting) individuals are present. Social skills programs often require strong listening comprehension skills and the capacity to translate verbally presented information into action. Good social skills training programs include modeling, so the target client must also be able to imitate skills. Perhaps most challenging is the capacity to generalize newly acquired social skills to all relevant situations in which they should be applied. It is impossible to fluently train every separate social skill that many be needed in every possible real world situation. Consider (1) every *discriminative stimulus* that signals a social skill should occur (plus every *S-delta* that signals it should not occur), (2) every *variant* of a social skill within a response class that may be appropriate or inappropriate and every way in which *execution* of the social skill may falter, as well as, (3) all *competing* rules that may govern the use or nonuse of every social skill. Given how dynamic social situations are and the number of factors that influence the generalizability of the social skills to pertinent situations, group social skills training programs will not be appropriate for all target clients who have social skill deficits. That is, group social skills training will not be appropriate for many individuals with ASD. Evidence-based practitioners need to give due consideration to the client's repertoire prior to treatment selection.

Assessment of client repertoire should occur on an ongoing basis and evidence-based practitioners should avoid the risk of making assumptions about client repertoire that would restrict the number of treatment options under consideration. For example, a treatment that was ineffective in the past should not be automatically rejected if the target client has acquired new skills because the news skills could impact treatment effectiveness. skillscould impact treatment effectiveness. The evidence-based practitioner asks, "Is the skill acquisition sufficient to reconsider using the treatment at this time?" Consider the case of Jaylen, a 20-year-old man with ASD whose new job is to sort mail in the workplace. His middle school teachers used video modeling to teach him to sort words and the treatment did not work. The evidence-based practitioner is familiar with this history and realizes that it is directly connected to the immediate task. Jaylen's history also shows that he had not mastered identification of letter sequences until high school. Video modeling was not appropriate in middle school because mastery of letter sequences was a prerequisite skill for sorting of words. Evidence-based practitioners consider target client repertoire—even for treatments that "failed" in the past.

BEHAVIORAL CUSPS

Behavioral cusps are behavior changes that have far-reaching effects because they significantly alter the target client's access to new environments (i.e., new contingencies, reinforcers and punishers, responses; Rosales-Ruiz & Baer, 1997). Practitioners often think about behavioral cusps when selecting which skills or behaviors should be targeted for change. Evidence-based practitioners also consider behavioral cusps when selecting which *intervention* is best. Practitioners can ask if exposure to the treatment itself could potentially serve as a behavioral cusp. For example, consider the case of Leah, a 7-year-old girl who is highly dependent on a paraprofessional for regulation of her activities at school. She is similarly dependent on her parents at home. In fact a primary parental concern is that they do not know what to do with Leah if she cannot be supervised (e.g., a parent is home alone and taking a shower or is sick). Young children who are more independent actually receive more intensive services and supports than children who are more dependent on others (McConnell, McEvoy, & Odom, 1992), so they have greater access to new environments. Next consider a few popular interventions that have strong evidence of effectiveness for increasing independence: Social Stories™ and Schedules. A Social Story™ typically identifies a target behavior and the environmental conditions that evoke and maintain the behavior, and are usually implemented in combination with other effective behavioral intervention procedures, such as reinforcement and prompt-fading. In this case the Social Story™ could explain the importance of completing tasks independently and the tasks described in the story could all be at mastery level. Alternatively, schedules involve the presentation of a series of activities in the order in which they should be completed. Schedules are often presented as pictures but may be posed as pictures combined with words or with words alone. "Which one would be better for Leah?" One of these treatments has a greater potential to lead to a behavioral cusp. A Social Story™ could increase independence with the tasks identified in the story. In fact, over time, additional tasks could be added or alternated in the story. This treatment might produce important changes in Leah's capacity to complete mastery level tasks independently—which sounds great! Schedules could accomplish this same goal. However, schedules could easily be moved over time from simple schedules to a comprehensive self-management system. That is, after mastering the schedule, Leah could be taught to evaluate whether or not she had completed the work to criterion herself, score her performance, and seek reinforcement for accurate, thorough, and independent completion of the series of tasks. The capacity to fully self-regulate in this way opens up many more opportunities over time and can be adapted to a wide range of tasks, including those that are not yet at mastery level. This analysis is not a disparagement of Social Stories™ as an intervention. Readers should know that I have conducted research on Social Stories™ and would advise using them in some cases. The purpose of this example is to show how evidence-based practitioners can consider different treatments in terms of their capacity to serve as behavioral cusps. Note that schedules are not any better at producing behavioral cusps than any other treatment if considerable planning is not put into place. Using schedules will not lead to a behavioral cusp if the evidence-based practitioner does not seriously plan each step of the change from schedules to self-management.

CHAPTER 5

Client Preferences

When two or more treatment options are viable, evidence-based practitioners consider what treatment is preferable to the target client. There are multiple strategies for using target client preference in the evidence-based practice (EBP) treatment selection process such as preference assessment, choice, and preference as a natural byproduct of treatment.

PREFERENCE ASSESSMENT

Preference assessments are completed to identify objects, attention, or activities that have a strong potential for serving as reinforcers for a target client. To truly serve this purpose, it is important to test out whether or not the identified preferences actually serve as reinforcers. There are ethical reasons to use preference assessments. Target clients have a right to provide consent for interventions and to be involved in the planning of their treatment (BACB, 2014). Furthermore, human beings have the legal right to reject treatments offered to them by any practitioner (behavior analysts, physicians, speech-language pathologists, etc.), as long as they are "mentally competent" (Standler, 2012). Although some individuals with ASD are not able to fully participate in this process due to their age or capacity, every possible opportunity to participate in decision-making should be offered. Preference assessment is one means for helping achieve this ethical goal and legal obligation. Furthermore, treatments are more acceptable when based on client preference (see chapter: Treatment Acceptability and Social Validity).

An exhaustive review of the preference assessment literature and methodology is beyond the scope of this practitioner's guide. However, interested readers are encouraged to read Virues-Ortega et al. (2014) for a recent literature review and decision-making model for selecting an appropriate preference assessment method for individuals with disabilities. Recent literature regarding nontraditional preference assessment methods are briefly highlighted below.

A Practical Guide to Finding Treatments That Work for People with Autism.
DOI: http://dx.doi.org/10.1016/B978-0-12-809480-8.00005-4

Group Administration

Preference can be determined for groups (e.g., in a classroom; Layer, Hanley, Heal, & Tiger, 2008) as well as individuals. The methodology used to assess preference in groups does, however, require specific skills to be within a client's repertoire. For example, children participating in the research on group administration of preference were capable of choosing a preferred stimulus from an array (e.g., multiple stimulus without replacement). In addition, they could participate in concurrent chains arrangements. For example, after first participating in an individual preference assessment, children were then taught to associate specific colors of paper with specific preference (e.g., blue equals cookies). This may not be a time-efficient process in many group settings and may not even be feasible when groups include individuals with more severe intellectual disabilities. Yet, for classrooms or other group situations in which this process is feasible, it may be more efficient over time. Similarly, these group preference assessments may be advisable in group homes where the same clients remain for protracted periods of time.

Infants and Toddlers

Earlier identification of ASD means strategies for assessing preference among infants and toddlers is necessary. The literature in this area is limited, but a review by Rush, Moretenson, and Birch (2010) provides many useful insights into how the existing preference assessment literature can be reasonably extended to this younger population. Below are a few examples:

- Practitioners should consider what skill sets are required for a client to participate in a preference assessment. For example, the capacity to make choices, demonstrate an adequate attention span, and a history of problem behaviors when access to objects are restricted can all impact the type of preference assessment that is completed.
- Satiation may quickly become a problem for younger children.
- Developmental considerations with respect to establishing operations must be examined. For example, a young child with ASD may not prefer a toy when he is left alone with it, but may find the toy highly preferable when another child uses the toy.

CHOICE

People are able to express their preferences whenever they are given a choice. Even very young children (both with and without disabilities) like to be given options (Brigham & Sherman, 1973; Fisher, Thompson,

Piazza, Crosland, & Gotjen, 1997; Tiger, Hanley, & Hernandez, 2006). Mastery of novel tasks can occur more quickly when individuals with disabilities are offered choice and people prefer to have the opportunity to make choices (Toussaint, Kodak, & Vladescu, 2016). Evidence-based practitioners can better meet their ethical obligations to involve clients in treatment planning when providing choice. However, client repertoire must be considered before choices are offered. For example, choice in research is often assessed by first identifying preferred consequences from an array and then participating in concurrent chains arrangements (Layer et al., 2008).

Individuals with ASD who have stronger communication skills can be asked what choices they would like to make. For example, if social skills are being targeted, the 13-year-old target client could be offered the options of (1) a social skills group that meets after school; (2) a peer-mediated social intervention (Peer Buddy) that pairs typically developing peers with a students on the spectrum; (3) Social Stories™, or (4) a community-based social skills program that is held on the weekends. The treatments would have to be fully explained along with the expectations for the target client. She would be asked to rank order the treatments and explain why this order is preferred. Her responses are:

1. The community-based social skills program on the weekend because school is pretty stressful and she does not want to stay at school any longer during the day.
2. The Peer Buddy program because it involves having a trusted friend at school but no extra hours at school.
3. Social Stories™ because she is "kind of bored" with these since they have been used with her for many years.
4. The after-school social skills program because she does not want to stay at school longer.

Generally speaking, whenever more than one evidence-based treatment option exists, the target client's choice should help guide the decision-making process. Highlighting target client choice will make it easier for evidence-based practitioners to take a less authoritarian attitude toward clients (Gambrill, 2001), which will strengthen the EBP process.

PREFERENCE AS A NATURAL BYPRODUCT OF TREATMENT

Preference can be a natural byproduct of treatment. For example, contingency contracting and environmental enrichment can each give the target client greater access to preferred objects or consequences simply as a result of being properly implemented.

Contingency Contracting

Contingency contracting is an intervention that involves identifying a behavior, the conditions under which the behavior is supposed to occur, and the consequences for both achieving the goal and failing to perform to a criterion. The target client collaborates with the practitioner to develop the contract and then signs the contract to indicate agreement with the contingencies outlined. Because the target client and the practitioner work together to specify relevant aspects of the contract, the target client is clearly involved in the planning and consent process. In addition, they can indicate their preferences related to the behavior, when it should occur, and the consequences for the behavior, so those preferences can be incorporated into the contract.

Environmental Enrichment

Environmental enrichment is typically used with clients who engage in higher rates of stereotypic behavior (e.g., hand flapping, rocking, toe walking). Environmental enrichment involves providing a large number of attractive materials (i.e., those that can be physically manipulated) in the target clients' environments (e.g., home, school, etc.). In this way the target client manipulates the toys or other objects instead of engaging in stereotypic behavior. This is a simple way to incorporate preference because clients are given increased access to materials they find engaging. Strong communication skills or the capacity to link abstract stimuli (e.g., different color paper) to specific preferences are not prerequisites for environmental enrichment. Thus there are options to include preference in some form for all target clients.

CHAPTER 6

Quality of Life, Generalization, and Social Validity

Social validity is the degree to which the target and stakeholder clients describe a treatment as fair, appropriate, and reasonable (Wolf, 1978). Social validity includes an evaluation of whether or not the (1) goals are socially important, (2) procedures are appropriate/acceptable; and (3) outcomes are meaningful. Issues of treatment appropriateness and acceptability are addressed in Chapter 7, Treatment Acceptability and Social Validity, but the issues of socially important goals and meaningful outcomes are addressed here in terms of quality of life (QoL) and generalization. When a number of evidence-based treatments are appropriate, evidence-based practitioners select those with higher social validity. Social validity is so important, in fact, that it should be discussed even when only one treatment option seems viable.

QUALITY OF LIFE

The concepts of socially important goals and socially meaningful outcomes are intertwined. You cannot produce meaningful changes in a target client's life unless the goal(s) of treatment are socially important. Each treatment option should be compared against this standard. Evidence-based practitioners determine which treatment option(s) will produce outcomes that change the target client's QoL. QoL is measured in four ways (Schalock, Gardner, & Bradley, 2007):

1. QoL is enhanced when target clients have the kinds of life experiences they prefer.
2. QoL is better when the target client lives a fuller life (e.g., are interconnected with important people in their lives and with their communities).
3. QoL is greater when physical and social well-being is improved within all relevant cultural environments.
4. QoL is better when target clients have experiences that are common to all human beings and are uniquely valued by the target client.

A Practical Guide to Finding Treatments That Work for People with Autism.
DOI: http://dx.doi.org/10.1016/B978-0-12-809480-8.00006-6

Practitioners serving the ASD and developmental disability populations have begun focusing on QoL not only for the target client but
also for the stakeholder clients (Boehm, Carter, & Taylor, 2015).
For example, family quality of life (FQoL) for transition age
(i.e., 18–21 years) individuals with ASD tend to be much higher when
problem behavior occurs at a low frequency (or not at all), when fewer
supports are needed, and when parents report a greater strength of
faith. Armed with this information, evidence-based practitioners
may discuss FQoL when selecting from among treatment options.
For example, evidence-based practitioners can help families prioritize
target behaviors/skills so that reasonable progress can be made
(i.e., often multiple target behaviors cannot be altered simultaneously
without sacrificing treatment fidelity). FQoL can be discussed in relation to other relevant stakeholder client variables (e.g., acceptability,
feasibility, etc.). That is, treatment targets can be prioritized in terms
of whether or not they are socially important and the treatment can
produce socially meaningful outcomes that impact the whole family.
In addition, researchers are beginning to examine whether or not
specific treatments can improve FQoL. Hopefully, researchers will
expand on the work of Buckley, Ente, and Ruef (2014) who have
provided preliminary evidence that Pivotal Response Training can
improve FQoL. However, evidence-based practitioners should not wait
for researchers to provide additional evidence before they incorporate
the evaluation of FQoL into the treatment selection as well as the
retention, adaptation, or rejection process.

GENERALIZATION

Another way of producing socially meaningful change is to ensure that
target skills are generalized across all relevant situations. It is hard to
say that QoL has been altered in a socially meaningful way if the client
with ASD cannot use the skill in real-world situations. Evidence-based
practitioners can plan for generalization, irrespective of the intervention they recommend. By ensuring that a behavior will be reduced or a
skill can be used across each relevant setting, the skill change is more
likely to produce socially meaningful changes. If the skill does not
have relevance across a range of settings, however, the target may
not be particularly socially meaningful. Evidence-based practitioners
are encouraged to review Stokes and Baer (1977) to identify all of the

ways they can work toward generalization. For example, to increase the likelihood a skill will be generalized across settings, it is best to use materials within a treatment protocol that are commonly used across environments (Stokes & Baer, 1977). Materials do not have to be exactly the same and it would be cumbersome to expect all stakeholder to purchase identical materials. However, similar materials that can be used across relevant settings can be used to enhance generalization.

In addition to planning for generalization *after* selecting a treatment, treatments can be selected: (1) on the basis of their transportability across settings, which will increase the likelihood of generalization, or (2) because generalization is more likely to be a natural by-product of the intervention (i.e., it may automatically result from the treatment). For example, script fading (i.e., written scripts that initially regulate social-communicative interactions but are then faded; appropriate non-scripted statements are reinforced) is a highly transportable intervention. As long as the communication skills needed in one situation appropriately apply to another situation, skills acquired through script fading are likely to generalize (Cowan & Allen, 2007). In addition, an intervention like Pivotal Response Treatment is designed to teach individuals with ASD to generalize new skills across relevant situations. This occurs because foundational aspects of Pivotal Response Treatment include teaching a child with ASD to respond to multiple cues within the environment (i.e., provide the appropriate response to a number discriminative stimuli that signal behavior that falls into the same response class; Suhrheinrich, Stahmer, & Schreibman, 2007) and to use self-management strategies (Koegel, Park, & Koegel, 2014). Stakeholder clients use natural reinforcers (another established strategy for increasing generalization; Stokes & Baer, 1977) and target pivotal skills (i.e., behavioral cusps that target positive outcomes; Koegel & Frea, 1993), which enhance the likelihood a skill will be used across relevant situations.

Generalization of skills with Pivotal Response Treatment may not be restricted to target clients. That is, stakeholder clients may also generalize the strategies they learn to situations that differ from the training environment. For example, parent—child interactions in real-world situations (that differ from the original training conditions) have been assessed when parents are exposed to either Pivotal

Response Treatment or an intervention that teaches skills sequentially. Parents who were taught to use skills sequentially did not improve their parent–child interactions during dinnertime. In contrast, collateral improvements occurred at dinnertime for parents taught Pivotal Response Treatment. Specifically, parental happiness, interest in their child's stress levels, and communication styles all improved after being trained to use Pivotal Response Treatment procedures (Koegel, Bimbela, & Schreibman, 1996). When parent or other stakeholder client skills are naturally used across a range of situations, the target client is likely to generalize their skills. Clearly, researchers need to examine more treatments in relation to FQoL and additional research should be conducted with Pivotal Response Treatment and other behavioral intervention procedures. In this way evidence-based practitioners can better select treatments that lead to both target and stakeholder client generalization.

CHAPTER 7

Treatment Acceptability and Social Validity

Treatment acceptability is an important form of social validity that involves answering five questions: "Is the treatment fair? . . .reasonable? . . .appropriate? . . .unintrusive? And would you recommend this treatment for others?" (Kazdin, 1980). Many tools that have adequate internal consistency and can be administered quickly have been developed to assess treatment acceptability. Different tools have been developed for parents, teachers, and children and these are described in Table 7.1. Clients must understand the treatment before acceptability can accurately be measured (Reimers, Wacker, & Koeppl, 1987). Evidence-based practitioners must ensure that all clients understand the treatments before completing treatment acceptability forms.

Many variables influence the likelihood a treatment will be deemed acceptable. Treatments using positive reinforcement-based procedures (e.g., praise, reinforcement, token economy) are more acceptable than treatments using punishment procedures (e.g., response cost, time-out). More complex treatments are less acceptable unless they are used to address more severe behavior (Elliott, Witt, Galvin, & Peterson, 1984). More time-intensive treatments are generally considered less acceptable by stakeholder clients (Elliott, Turco, Evans, & Gresham, 1984). However, this does not mean that parents, teachers, or other care providers are unwilling to implement treatments that require more time. It means that evidence-based practitioners need to provide a strong rationale for why a more time-intensive treatment may be recommended and listen to stakeholder clients concerns even after these reasons have been offered. Treatments that are less restrictive are also viewed as more acceptable (and they are associated with a higher QoL).

Views about treatment acceptability might be influenced by membership in different cultural groups (Wilczynski, Henderson, Harris, Bostic, & Kosmala, in press). Mothers' rate treatments are more acceptable for behavioral interventions when their children demonstrate severe behavior (Miller & Kelley, 1992), but fathers' report

A Practical Guide to Finding Treatments That Work for People with Autism.
DOI: http://dx.doi.org/10.1016/B978-0-12-809480-8.00007-8

Table 7.1 Commonly Used Treatment Acceptability Instruments

Instrument	Description	Internal Consistency	Target Audience
Treatment Evaluation Inventory (TEI; Kazdin, 1980)	• Developed for children with behavior disorders • A 15-item questionnaire • Targets concerns regarding treatment procedures • Relatively brief to administer • Uses a 7-point Likert-type scale	Ranges from 0.35 to 0.96	• Parents • Used primarily in research studies
Treatment Evaluation Inventory-Short Form (TEI-SF; Kelley, Heffer, Gresham, & Elliott, 1989)	• Short version of TEI • A 9-item questionnaire • Targets concerns regarding treatment procedures • Brief to administer • Uses a 5-point Likert-type scale	0.85	• Parents
Treatment Acceptability Rating Form (TARF; Reimers & Wacker, 1988)	• Developed based on TEI but for clinical settings • A 15-item questionnaire • Targets concerns regarding treatment procedures, costs, perceived effectiveness • Relatively brief to administer • Uses a 7-point Likert-type scale	Ranges from 0.80 and 0.91	• Parents • Used for clinical settings
Treatment Acceptability Rating Form Revised. (TARF-R; Reimers, Wacker, & Cooper, 1991)	• Expanded version of TARF • A 20-item questionnaire • Targets concerns about treatment, problem severity, and understanding of treatment. • Relatively brief to administer • Uses a 7-point Likert-type scale	0.92	• Parents • Used for clinical settings
Intervention Rating Profile* (Tarnowski & Simonian, 1992)	• Developed for use in educational settings. • A 20-item questionnaire • Targets concerns about acceptability, risk to the client, amount of time treatment requires, effects on other students, and teach skill • Relatively brief to administer • Uses a 6-point Likert-type scale	0.89	• Teachers • Used for educational settings
Intervention Rating Profile 15 (IRP-15; Martens, Witt, Elliott, & Darveaux, 1985)	• Brief version of IRP • A 15-item questionnaire • Targets concerns about acceptability, feasibility, and perceived effectiveness • Relatively brief to administer • Uses a 6-point Likert-type scale	0.98	• Teachers • Used for educational settings
The Children's Intervention Rating Profile (CIRP; Witt & Elliott, 1985)	• A 7-item questionnaire • Modification of IRP • Targets fairness and expected effectiveness of treatment • Readability: 5th grade level • Uses a 7-point Likert-type scale	Ranges from 0.75 to 0.89 Less internal consistency than adult measures	• Child, Students

(Continued)

Table 7.1 (Continued)			
Instrument	Description	Internal Consistency	Target Audience
The Behavior Intervention Rating Scale (BIRS; Elliott & Von Brock Treuting, 1991)	• A 24-item questionnaire • Modification of the IRP-15 • Uses a 6-point Likert-type scale	0.97	• Parent • Teachers
Abbreviated Acceptability Rating Profile (AARP; Tarnowski & Simonian, 1992)	• Modification of IRP-15 • An 8-item questionnaire • Uses a 6-point Likert-type scale	Ranges from 0.89 to 0.98	• Parents

Note: *All instruments are scored by summing responses; higher scores indicate greater treatment acceptability.*

medical interventions are more acceptable than mothers. However, marital status, age, and income are unrelated to treatment acceptability (Dahl, Tervo, & Symons, 2007). Parents perceptions about support (e.g., tangible and emotional) from immediate and extended family members have also been associated with higher treatment acceptability (Pemberton & Borrego, 2005).

The behavior of the practitioner recommending a treatment influences treatment acceptability (Spreat & Walsh, 1994). A treatment is considered more acceptable when practitioners use pragmatic language instead of professional jargon (Witt, Moe, Gutkin, & Andrews, 1984). Jargon allows practitioners from the same discipline to efficiently communicate with each other, but it may create barriers when communicating with professionals from other disciplines or with lay persons. Practitioners can use jargon without realizing it. For example, making the statement, "He is engaging in tantrum behavior," is awkward and potentially off-putting to a parent or an educator. In contrast, saying, "He is tantrumming" more effectively communicates the present challenge. Ethically the practitioner needs to ensure that the technology not only remains sufficiently rigorous to produce the intended outcome but also must explain the treatment to target and stakeholder clients using accessible language (BACB, 2014).

Practitioners should include target clients' perspective about treatment acceptability whenever they are capable of participating in the evaluation. Children tend to rate all treatments as less acceptable than adults do (Kazdin, French, & Sherick, 1981); however, differences in children's views about treatment acceptability have emerged in the literature. Some research has shown that girls view group contingencies as less acceptable, particularly as problem severity for an individual child is greater (Elliott et al., 1984). In addition, some research has shown that black children find group contingencies more acceptable than white children (Elliott et al., 1984).

There are methodological weaknesses in the treatment acceptability literature that limit its usefulness to evidence-based practitioners. For example, many research participants and/or their parents/teachers drop out of a clinical study either before or during treatment. If the researchers ask the remaining participants about treatment acceptability, they may report an inflated level of acceptability for a given treatment. However, one reason that participants drop out of research is because the treatment is not acceptable. For example, in a study on cognitive behavioral treatment, almost half (46.7%) of participants dropped out of the study due to low motivation or dissatisfaction with the treatment or the therapist (Bados, Balaguer, & Saldana, 2007). Practitioners may question the value of collecting treatment acceptability data when even researchers have difficulty accurately assessing it. But evidence-based practitioners should be motivated to collect treatment acceptability data for a number of reasons. First, if researchers lose a large number of research participants because the target and stakeholder clients are not happy with the treatment, practitioners are also likely to have clients drop out of the same treatment. If for no other reason, there is an immediate economic impact on practitioners who lose up to half of their clients! Treatment acceptability data can be collected prior to or during treatment implementation. Second, practitioners have an ethical obligation to involve target and stakeholder clients when they are planning treatments (BACB, 2014). Treatment acceptability is an essential way to involve clients in the EBP treatment selection process. It would be an ethical violation to ignore the fact that the target and/or stakeholder clients find the treatment unacceptable (or less acceptable than reasonable and equally effective alternate treatments). Third, once a treatment has been implemented, practitioners have an obligation to continue involving target and stakeholder clients before significant changes are made to the program (BACB, 2014) and assessing treatment acceptability is a one aspect of meeting this obligation. Fourth, scholars have argued that treatment acceptability is directly tied to treatment fidelity. Researchers have not conclusively demonstrated whether or not this is true (Mautone et al., 2009; Sterling-Turner & Watson, 2002). However, treatment acceptability should be assessed simply because it could improve treatment fidelity.

Accurate assessment of treatment acceptability requires more than a questionnaire. Evidence-based practitioners must convey that they sincerely care about and would make treatment selection decisions based on the information that is shared. Stakeholder clients may wish to please the practitioner or they may fear that their relationship with the practitioner could be compromised if concerns are shared. Clients will share their beliefs about treatment acceptability only if they are convinced that there will not be negative consequences for doing so.

A final indicator of treatment acceptability is the continuation of services. Target and stakeholder clients have the right to refuse a treatment approach (Detrich, 1999) and the right to discontinue services altogether. Continuation of services is, however, a simplistic assessment of acceptability because many target and stakeholder clients have a tremendous need for services. As a result, other practitioners may not be available to provide services (Vivanti et al., 2014), so they continue treatment out of desperation even though they find it to unacceptable. Therefore evidence-based practitioners are wise to use this information as only a gross indicator of treatment acceptability and the services they provide.

CHAPTER 8

Treatment Feasibility and Social Validity

A treatment cannot be socially valid if it cannot actually be implemented. That is, socially meaningful improvements can only result when a treatment is accurately and feasibly put in place. A treatment might be ideal in all other regards (e.g., evidence, preference), but if it is not feasible, the target client will never actually access the intervention. Treatment feasibility represents the capacity to accurately implement a treatment in real-world situations. If a treatment cannot be accurately and practically implemented in real-world settings, it may produce beautiful data on journal pages, but it will not produce meaningful changes in clients' lives. Thus treatments that are not feasible are also not socially valid. Indicators of feasibility identified by researchers include treatment acceptability, demand for the services, treatment fidelity, practicality, adaptability, and integration (i.e., the range of system-level changes that are necessary to implement/maintain this intervention; Bowen et al., 2009; Pugliese & White, 2014). Acceptability has already been addressed in Chapter 7, Treatment Acceptability and Social Validity. For the purpose of this chapter, we will break all of the remaining aspects of feasibility into three categories: resource constraint, environmental support, and fidelity. The issue of context will be addressed in this chapter.

Evidence-based practitioners consider all relevant potential obstacles prior to selecting treatments. Costs are the most apparent obstacle, but many barriers are not directly related to cost. "Are there additional expectations of staff?" "What kind of environmental changes are needed and how will this impact all stakeholders?," "What skill sets will be required of stakeholder clients (e.g., if you want them to collect data, have you done everything possible to train them and have you simplified data collection)?" These are just a few of the questions evidence-based practitioners ask all relevant parties, including parents, teachers, center directors, and target clients (when they are capable of participating in these discussions) prior to making a treatment decision.

A Practical Guide to Finding Treatments That Work for People with Autism.
DOI: http://dx.doi.org/10.1016/B978-0-12-809480-8.00008-X

RESOURCE CONSTRAINT

Resources are needed to implement treatments (Albin, Lucyshyn, Horner, & Flannery, 1996; Detrich, 1999; Wacker et al., 1990), and evidence-based practitioners determine what resources are needed for each treatment under consideration. Immediate material costs are required for each treatment. However, staffing needs represent a tremendous budgetary demand (Detrich, 1999). The individual responsible for paying for the treatment may be more keenly aware and concerned about this cost than the average practitioner. This may be particularly relevant when intensive resources are required to sustain treatments over a long period of time. Evidence-based practitioners learn about the funding source for materials and training costs. They realize approval for funding may require a good deal of red tape and time. As a result, a treatment that might be effective and ideal for all other reasons may not be the best solution at the current time if it is too resource intensive, particularly if there are other equally effective but less resource-intensive options. A treatment might be feasible only in the long term and an alternate intervention may be needed in the interim.

ENVIRONMENTAL SUPPORTS

Treatments are often much less effective when transported from highly controlled research setting to real-world settings (Weisz, Jensen-Doss, & Hawley, 2006). This outcome may be due, in part, to the fact that clients seen in real-world settings are often more complex than those who typically participate in research. Researchers often exclude participants who have comorbid diagnoses so they can clearly show a treatment works for a specific population. In addition, real-world settings are typically more dynamic (i.e., more complex and less controlled) than research conditions. In real life, parents, teachers, allied health professionals, and direct care staff must figure out how to select the best treatment in more complex situations and with clients who are more complicated.

Environmental supports are any variables that enhance or undermine the capacity to implement an intervention in real-world settings, with the exception of costs. Environmental supports vary tremendously across different situations, settings, and contexts. Treatments are not implemented in a vacuum—they are implemented within a culture. The cultural unit may be the family, the school, the group home, the hospital, or any other community-based setting. Each culture will have its own unique features that can influence whether or not a treatment is feasible. For that reason, the supports that are more likely to impact families, educators, and other professionals are addressed separately. However, any of these variables may be relevant in all settings.

Families

Families do their own cost−benefit analyses before authorizing or implementing a treatment. Although costs enter into the equation, parents must determine if a treatment is practical for their child and the whole family. When parents make decisions about adopting a treatment, they must consider the burden the treatment will put on all family members (Dahl, Tervo, & Symons, 2007). This aspect of feasibility is directly connected to family quality of life. Parents consider the time commitments required of them, particularly when the treatment necessitates a high degree of parental involvement (Karst & Van Hecke, 2012). When their response effort is high or when the outcomes are delayed with a low guarantee for meaningful change, parents may not select an intervention (Allen & Warzak, 2000).

One indicator of treatment feasibility is how "engaged" parents are in the treatment process (Pugliese & White, 2014). For example, "if the parents are active members of the treatment team, are they completing therapy with their child?," "Are they regularly attending trainings so that treatment fidelity can be achieved and/or maintained?" When problems with attendance or engagement are evident, the evidence-based practitioner reassesses feasibility by discussing barriers to implementation and treatment acceptability with the family. Families may wish to implement a given intervention, but in reality, it is not viable given the other demands on their budget and time. Evidence-based practitioners make decisions about the appropriateness of an intervention and adapt or reject treatments so target client goals are achieved without adding significant stress to the family system.

When given the chance to share their concerns about feasibility, parents provide great insight about the environmental supports that are important to them. For example, working parents who participated in a parent training program reported concerns about childcare and said it had direct bearing on their capacity to fully participate. They were concerned about being clearly informed about the commitments required prior to initiating treatment. Parents said being given resources that were appropriate for parents (e.g., avoided jargon, were brief, etc.) and having enough time spent focusing on the issues that were critical to them increased the value of training (Dababnah & Parish, 2016). By sincerely asking parents about all aspects of environmental supports, families are more likely to fully participate in the treatment selection process, and possibly, intervention implementation. Evidence-based practitioners address barriers to feasibility to achieve this goal.

Educators

In school cultures, interactions between adults and students are adult-directed. That is, teachers, paraprofessionals, or other adults tell students what to do and students are expected to comply with adults' directives. However, some effective treatments are inconsistent with this culture. Treatments will be viewed as more acceptable and feasible when they have greater similarity with the treatments that are currently in place (Albin et al., 1996). Thus a naturalistic treatment that is child-directed may not be deemed feasible because it is so discrepant from the cultural expectations and existing treatments (Detrich, 1999).

Evidence-based practitioners can learn much about treatment feasibility from researchers who have attempted to translate research from highly controlled laboratories into real-world settings. Researchers investigating treatment adoption asked the following questions:

- "Is the treatment is acceptable?"
- "What previous experiences do the stakeholders have with a treatment?"
- "Do stakeholders have favorable attitudes about the treatment?"
- "What is the level of stakeholder excitement/resistance to adopting the new treatment?" (Kolko, Hoagwood, & Springgate, 2010)

The reasons many teachers do not consistently use empirically supported treatments (Hendricks, 2011) are directly related to feasibility. Teachers often do not receive sufficient instruction in their teacher preparation programs at universities to allow them to implement these interventions (Morrier, Hess, & Heflin, 2011). Furthermore, most teachers do not receive behavioral skills training that would allow them to accurately implement these sometimes complex interventions

(Fixsen, Blasé, Naoom, & Wallace, 2009). Evidence-based practitioners should not assume that teachers have had training that would reasonably be expected to lead to treatment fidelity. For example, didactic instruction is insufficient unless it is also paired with competency-based training and coaching. When complex treatments that require extensive training are under consideration, evidence-based practitioners may need to develop an immediate and long-term plan. The immediate plan could involve a treatment that can be accurately implemented immediately. A long-term plan could be developed, so that teachers could receive sufficient training to help them develop the requisite skills for high levels of treatment fidelity. Evidence-based practitioners must develop a comprehensive strategy to build long-term capacity and progress monitoring toward this goal is imperative. Capacity building applies equally across all stakeholder groups.

Allied Health Providers and Direct Care Staff

The exact protocol that produced gains in well-funded research may not be feasible when evidence-based practitioners provide services to complicated clients in other treatment settings. Although it might be necessary to adapt the ideal treatment (Weisz, Jenson-Doss, & Hawley, 2006), the smallest deviation from the effective research supported protocol that is still sensitive to target client and stakeholder client variables (e.g., feasibility) is ideal. Just as with parents and teachers, evidence-based practitioners may need to overcome challenges to feasibility in centers, community-based agencies, or healthcare settings by using the following strategies:

- Look closely at the training required to get clinicians/supervisors to implement the treatment with fidelity. More extensive training (e.g., behavioral skills training) is typically necessary when developing and maintaining implementation accuracy.
- Identify potential barriers to implementation and problem-solve around those concerns. Each situation may be unique. For example, a group home could be staffed with a large number of employees for whom English is a Second Language, so training may need to be adapted to allow staff more time to process what is being said to them. Similarly, a hospital could have a lot of shift workers and scheduling of training may need to be more flexible (e.g., repeated training opportunities, being sensitive to the schedules of staff and the clients they serve).

- Identify and problem-solve potential barriers to sustainability. For example, turnover of direct care staff may be greatest in an autism center when local schools provide higher salaries and better benefits for paraprofessionals. As a result, training may need to be scheduled more frequently so new staff can accurately implement the intervention. Similarly, a community-based employment program might support target clients in a wide range of workplace settings and the tasks assigned to target clients might vary considerably. Generalizing and sustaining the interventions across workplace environments will probably require more staff coaching.

ADDRESSING RESOURCE CONSTRAINT/ENVIRONMENTAL SUPPORTS

Determining treatment feasibility is not a unidirectional discussion. That is, although evidence-based practitioners should initiate a discussion about all of the variables that could serve as barriers to accurate implementation, they should also facilitate a discussion about the strategies that can be used to overcome these challenges. The purpose of the discussion is not to convince stakeholder clients to adopt a treatment, but rather, to help them develop practical solutions to barriers they would face if a preferred treatment were selected. During this process, evidence-based practitioners should learn what factors motivate stakeholders to adopt a new treatment. The evidence-based practitioner identifies strategies for reducing the level of response effort a parent needs to exert (e.g., "Can they hire staff to complete some of the tasks?") or accessing incentives for a teacher to participate in performance feedback/coaching. Evidence-based practitioners recognize that human beings tend to avoid the unknown. Rather than describing procedures in a sterile manner, evidence-based practitioners talk about what it will mean to implement the intervention in realistic terms. Identifying how a given treatment could impact the transportation needs of the family or how hard it can be to see a child upset when treatments are first put in place shows the stakeholder client that you appreciate the challenges they may be facing. It is also important to ask if the solutions that are being generated seem realistic and manageable given the other demands on the stakeholder client. The goal is to select the best treatment for the target client based on the real-world settings and situation. By taking the time to discuss how a treatment will actually fit into stakeholder clients lives, the likelihood of identifying the treatment that best fits the target and stakeholder clients will increase (Kolko et al., 2010).

The issue of implementation accuracy must be included in any discussion that evidence-based practitioners have with stakeholder clients (Kolko et al., 2010). When stakeholder clients are concerned that they will not be able to implement a treatment with a high degree of accuracy, evidence-based practitioners either continue problem-solving or they determine that the treatment is not best at this time. However, it is possible to systematically remove barriers over time, so the intervention does not have to be placed on the permanent "unfeasible" list. Evidence-based practitioners also identify barriers to sustaining the treatment for the length of time necessary to produce benefits. If a stakeholder client is capable of implementing the intervention, but the supports needed to do so will not be regularly available, further problem-solving is needed. For example, a father may say he can coordinate the staff needed to implement early intensive behavioral intervention at this point in time, but this will present a problem when he finds a job. The evidence-based practitioner should discuss how the family might overcome this barrier or if they should seek services from an autism center who can coordinate these services. The treatment might still be "right" for the target client and family, but the conditions under which it is delivered might be different. The level of behavioral skills training/coaching that will be needed may also influence treatment selection decisions.

The "right" treatment might involve a short-term intervention that can be easily implemented immediately and a long-term treatment that the evidence-based practitioner and the stakeholder client work toward until a high degree of treatment fidelity can be attained. The convenience of training and coaching might also be a barrier to treatment feasibility (Kolko et al., 2010), and evidence-based practitioners must be creative in identifying cost-effective and time-efficient training options. Sometimes, knowledge about someone who is a local champion for a given intervention is beneficial. For example, in a school system, a teacher assistance team may have a team member who has significant training and has implemented the intervention previously. They might not only advocate for the treatment but also provide local supports, thus improving cost effectiveness.

TREATMENT FIDELITY

Treatment fidelity has been referenced throughout this practitioner's guide. Treatment fidelity reflects the extent to which an intervention is accurately implemented, but this requires multiple components. Treatment fidelity requires that the treatment is implemented: (1) correctly; (2) consistently for all clients; (3) consistently across the entire time the treatment is needed (Smith, Daunic, & Tayler, 2007). Treatment fidelity can also include quality and dosage of implementation (Power et al., 2005; Sanetti & Kratochwill, 2009). Treatment integrity, implementation accuracy, and procedural accuracy are all terms that essentially describe the assessment of how well a treatment was implemented as designed. Treatment fidelity is important because it is impossible to know how to proceed if a treatment does not work for a given client when the treatment was not accurately delivered.

Treatment fidelity data can also identify whether or not a treatment is feasible in real-world settings. For example, a teacher may not have enough supports in the classroom to implement a treatment with fidelity. Public school teachers often report that they receive inadequate training, so their expertise in serving children with ASD may be insufficient (Jennett, Harris, & Mesibov, 2003). In addition, teachers often supply some of the materials they need to provide standard educational services in schools. Their commitment to their students is not the problem—but access to sufficient resources may be. Treatment fidelity tends to be low for the following reasons:

1. There are inadequate tangible resources (resource constraint).
2. The treatment requires too much response effort (environmental support).
3. The stakeholder clients responsible for implementing the treatment have received insufficient training and coaching (environmental support).
4. Systemic level supports are not available (resource constraint or environmental support).
5. Although stakeholder clients agreed to implement the intervention, in reality they do not find the treatment acceptable and do not accurately implement the treatment. This may occur because the treatment adoption decision was made by leader clients (treatment acceptability) or because the treatment is different in practice than they had imagined during training.

6. The target client rarely comes in contact with the treatment because it does not appropriately match their needs (e.g., client is so aggressive that he spends tremendous time with reductive procedures instead of the planned treatment protocol; "best" treatment was not selected).

Treatment fidelity in the natural environment is much harder to accomplish than fidelity for research purposes (Noell et al., 2014). Not only are clients more complex, but also some stakeholder clients may not have received sufficient training to implement a treatment with fidelity. For example, teachers can implement a range of behavioral strategies (e.g., discrete trial training, pivotal response training, teaching within functional routines) when they receive extensive training, coaching, and time to develop and maintain skills (Stahmer et al., 2015). This raises many feasibility questions, however. "What are the costs associated with this level of training?," "How much time is needed to produce proficiency?," "How long will external trainers be needed to develop and maintain these skills?," "What resources will have to be reallocated, so teachers can attend training and coaching while their students are still being educated?" Even when these questions are answered, it is important to realize that more complex treatments that require greater clinical decision-making (e.g., pivotal response training) may still require more efforts to produce fidelity (Stahmer et al., 2015).

Another challenge with sustained treatment fidelity is procedural drift (also known as therapist drift). Procedural drift involves a deviation from the originally high level of implementation accuracy that occurred at the onset of intervention (Waller, 2009) or when treatment fidelity weakens despite the fact that adequate resources are available (Waller & Turner, 2016). Procedural drift has consistently been a problem across a range of professionals or family members who implement interventions. For example, stakholder clients who initially have high levels of treatment fidelity immediately following training can show significant drops in implementation accuracy within a few weeks (Sanetti & Kratochwill, 2009). To sustain treatment fidelity, ongoing coaching may be needed. The cost of ongoing coaching and the additional effort that is required on the part of the stakeholder client may mean the intervention is unsustainable.

A variety of methods have been used to increase treatment fidelity and often more than one method is used sequentially. For example, in some studies, participants take and pass a written exam before completing 5 days of applied practice. The treatment is then delivered in the natural setting using the same treatment fidelity checklists (Lopata, Toomey, et al., 2015). This comprehensive approach to enhancing treatment fidelity may not be feasible in many settings, particularly when there is not enough money to support this level of effort on the part of the trainees. However, useful strategies for improving implementation accuracy can be gleaned from this process. First, operational definitions paired with a task analysis can improve treatment fidelity (Gresham, MacMillan, Beebe-Frankenberger, & Bocian, 2000). Second, careful assessment of the necessary competencies is needed to implement the treatment accurately. Third, treatment fidelity can be improved when practitioners build rapport with stakeholder clients. Fourth, expert and/or consumer evaluation of the consistency of training across trainers, occasions, and sessions can improve treatment fidelity (Hennessey & Rumrill, 2003).

Some stakeholders have already been trained on a given treatment, but not all training methods are equally effective. Although didactic training can improve knowledge about a treatment, it is insufficient for developing procedural acquisition of skills (Dufrene, Lestremau, & Zoder-Martell, 2014). Didactic instruction can be an important part of training because it is difficult to accurately perform a complex procedure without sufficiently understanding the technique. Yet this didactic instruction must be supplemented with performance feedback and behavioral skills training. Performance feedback involves collaboration between the practitioner and the stakeholder client. The evidence-based practitioner acknowledges and praises accurate implementation of treatment components. The combination of feedback and praise explain why fidelity can improve so significantly (Kaufman, Codding, Markus, & Nagler, 2013) with performance feedback. When performance deviates from the behavior plan, constructive feedback is delivered and the components of treatment are reviewed in sequence. In addition the components in which an error occurred are rehearsed and immediate feedback is delivered until the stakeholder client can confidently and accurately deliver the intervention. Lastly, treatment fidelity data are graphed and shared with the stakeholder client using language that makes the graph meaningful. Collectively, this process allows the stakeholder client to see their improvements and to be supported as they develop complex skills (McKenney & Brisol, 2014). Behavioral skills training involves the same processes as performance feedback; however, modeling is combined with all of the described components of the performance feedback in order to increase skill acquisition and treatment fidelity (Gianoumis, Seiverling, & Sturmey, 2012). Stakeholder clients need to be provided sufficient opportunities to practice to a criterion (Sarver, Beidel, & Spitalnick, 2014), so evidence-based practitioners should intersperse modeling, opportunities to practice, and feedback.

Treatment Acceptability

Treatment acceptability has already been described in Chapter 7, Treatment Acceptability and Social Validity, in a section about target clients. It is referenced here as a reminder that treatment acceptability data should be collected from all relevant stakeholder clients and their views about treatment acceptability should be incorporated into the treatment selection decision. As with target client treatment acceptability, a treatment that has the potential to be effective should still be deprioritized if it is unacceptable to stakeholder clients. This decision should only occur after the evidence-based practitioner facilitates a conversation that is sensitive to their concerns.

Sustainability

A final consideration with respect to stakeholder client views is the issue of sustainability. Evidence-based practitioners should determine the likelihood a treatment can be sustained for the duration necessary to produce the desired outcomes. For example, if a family selects early intensive behavioral intervention as an option but they either cannot implement it at the dosage needed to produce change or for the period of time typically required to produce the expected level of benefit, the treatment may not be appropriate. If stakeholder clients believe a treatment is likely to result in "recovery" (defined as the remediation of deficits across all developmental domains) but this is virtually impossible because the treatment cannot be sustained sufficiently, the evidence-based practitioner is facing an ethical quagmire and alternate interventions are necessary.

CHAPTER 9

Context Matters: Getting Systems to Adopt Treatments

Decisions about adopting a treatment may not be made by the stakeholder client, who is often responsible for implementing the intervention. Superintendents, school principals, special education directors, or center directors are "leader clients" who often determine that their staff should be trained how to use a given treatment. The term "leader client" has been selected because evidence-based practitioners should not lose sight of the fact that these organizational leaders are members of the client group. Leader clients consider issues of immediate feasibility and sustainability on a systemic level (as compared to individual costs and supports needed to maintain an intervention for a given client). For example, special education teachers only remain in the field, on an average, from 3 to 5 years (Futernick, 2007). Given the turnover rate in special education, teachers in these settings often have limited experience, which can impact the capacity to implement highly complex treatment protocols. One of the greatest challenges to implementation of empirically supported treatments in real-world settings is treatment complexity (Stahmer et al., 2015). If a treatment is extremely complex and requires expert clinical decision-making to be effective, these leader clients may reject recommendations even if they have strong research support. Similarly, a community-based program that relies on one qualified professional who manages inexperienced direct care staff who graduated from high school only a year or two before may not be positioned to implement a complex treatment. Evidence-based practitioners ask leader clients many questions about feasibility because it may be necessary to develop both immediate and long-term treatment plans to best serve target clients. For example, a simpler treatment may be most appropriate in the immediate (e.g., differential reinforcement-based system) while a plan for long-term treatment (e.g., early intensive behavioral intervention) is developed and put into place. Also, evidence-based practitioners can help leader clients realize that staff turnover may be reduced

A Practical Guide to Finding Treatments That Work for People with Autism.
DOI: http://dx.doi.org/10.1016/B978-0-12-809480-8.00009-1

when adequate training has been provided (Aarons, Somerfeld, Hecht, Silovsky, & Chaffin, 2009).

Autism centers, community mental health agencies, health service agencies, and community-based programs are each distinctive settings that face unique situations, in part, as a result of the organizational structure and the climate that is established by leader clients. New treatments have the potential to have a profound impact on the larger organizational system. Organizations may be more important for long-term success than stakeholder clients (Rousseau, 1977). Although organizational leaders may not be involved when a decision is made to adopt a treatment for a given client, they have a strong and broad impact when treatment adoption decisions are made for the organization as a whole. Evidence-based practitioners may focus on individual clients, but they should be concerned about systemic adoption of a treatment because these decisions may impact the feasibility of the intervention for their client. Furthermore, leader clients may determine that resources or environmental supports will or will not be available at the individual client level. Organizational leaders conduct a cost–benefit analysis that is broadly conceived. For example, principals or center directors may ask these questions (and many more):

- "Will new collaborative partnerships be needed?"
- "If new collaborative partnerships are built, is the partner willing, capable, and respectful?"
- "What new demands will be placed on leaders (i.e., leader response effort)?"
- "How are the relationships with clients impacted?"
- "How feasible will it be to implement the intervention in this setting?"
- "What resources will be needed to be implement the intervention?," "Can resources be reallocated within the organization?," "Is the treatment cost-effective?"
- "What staffing resources will be needed and can these be managed within the existing budget?"
- "What funding sources may be needed if existing staffing and materials resources are not within the budget?," "How will these funding sources be accessed?"
- "How generalizable will the treatment methods be to other clients?"
- "Will the treatment methods be compatible with the existing cultural norms?"

Note: These questions were largely adapted from the Australian Children's Education & Care Quality Authority: Guide to the National Quality Standard; McHugh & Barlow, 2012; and Sarver, Beidel, and Spitalnick (2014).

Leaders' intention to adopt an intervention center around three broad factors: (1) expected value, which is based, in part on effectiveness; (2) perception of the treatment in relation to social norms; and (3) the capacity to implement the intervention, including availability of resources, transportability to the organization, capacity to overcome barriers, and the readiness of the organization to adopt the intervention (Backer, David, & Soucy, 1995; Schoenwald, McHugh, & Barlow, 2012).

Pyramidal training may be an option that keeps costs down and builds local expertise. Pyramidal training, also known as train-the-trainers model, involves training a small number of staff who can subsequently train additional staff. In this way the organization can develop staff skills that can be used with other clients with ASD (Pence, St. Peter, & Tetreault, 2012) and reduce the concern for turnover. Evidence-based practitioners also talk with leader clients about scheduling training at a time that works for the entire organization and uses innovative methods for delivering supports (e.g., use of web-based training for knowledge when feasible and web-based coaching that is electronically secure). Leader clients should also be encouraged to share follow-up assessments that would satisfy any concerns about staff who have been trained to criterion. In this way evidence-based practitioners can show the leader client they value concerns the leader client may have for the organization.

Implementing treatments in real-world settings requires careful attention to the attitudes of relevant members of an organization (Kolko, Hoagwood, & Springgate, 2010), which includes organizational leader clients. Leader client attitudes may be influenced through several means. Peers may identify the value, effectiveness, or utility of an intervention. They may communicate with each other about the challenges they face and solutions to those difficulties. Leader clients can influence each other's perspective about whether or not a treatment should be adopted. In addition, mass media can influence a leader's decision to adopt a treatment. Stories about autism treatments are regularly in the media. Some stories portray treatments as highly effective or extremely dangerous and media representation may not be accurate. These media stories do not have to be accurate to impact adoption decisions. Finally the communication style of the person advocating for a given treatment is likely to have a strong impact on the likelihood a treatment will be implemented (Rogers, 2003). The following will serve as red flags for leaders who are considering whether or not to adopt a treatment. Evidence-based practitioners should avoid:

- Using technical jargon unnecessarily because practitioners may be perceived as being unable to effectively communicate with professionals within the organizational system.
- Stating that only one treatment option should be considered because practitioners may be viewed as uninformed.
- Disregarding the relevance of financial costs, staff needs, or other barriers to feasibility because practitioners are less likely to be taken seriously.
- Communicating in a way that increases discord among stakeholder and leader clients because the practitioner is less likely to be viewed as part of the solution.
- Being unprepared to discuss the amount of time and ongoing training required to develop staff implementation skills because practitioners may be viewed as naïve.
- Demonstrating ignorance about organizational challenges, rules/ regulations, and the culture because practitioners are likely to be dismissed as unreliable sources of information.

Evidence-based practitioners consider the interconnectedness of all leader client concerns. For example, leader clients are often concerned about resources and staff burnout/turnover. The issue of burnout among special education teachers is even greater than general education teachers (Boe, Bobbitt, & Cook, 1997) so the concern is both very real and can have a significant impact on the organization (e.g., students do not consistently receive supports from experienced teachers). Special education teachers are under tremendous stress due to unmanageable workloads, excessive paperwork, and lack of resources (Fore, Martin, & Bender, 2002). In fact, teacher burnout may be connected to the current teacher shortage (Billingsley, 2004). The evidence-based practitioner may share with leader clients that teachers who have access to appropriate resources and training may be better able to cope with the challenges of teaching (Cherniss, 1995), so burnout and turn-over may be diminished.

Evidence-based practitioners recognize that the pure adoption of a treatment may not occur. Leader clients must manage a broad range of contextual issues and treatment selection is not dictated to the leader client. Adaptation of the intervention may be necessary (Chorpita & Nakamura, 2004). Collaboration between the evidence-based practi-tioner, stakeholder clients, leader clients (or their designee) will be needed to properly adapt the treatment in a way that reflects resource constraint, environmental supports, and contextual factors while main-taining a high degree of treatment fidelity.

Evidence-based practitioners need to clarify the scope of work required to produce changes, link the proposed interventions directly to the target client's improvements, demonstrate a collaborative approach with all organizational staff (including leader clients), help create organizational supports if this is desired, and ensure recommen-dations are feasible for the target and stakeholder clients as well as the context (Gersten, Vaughn, Deshler, & Schiller, 1997). Whenever speak-ing with leader clients, the goals of their organization should influence how treatments are discussed. For example, when proposing a new intervention to an ABA Autism center, behavioral jargon can be used, but outcomes should be described in terms of helping clients meet their behavioral goals. In contrast, when discussing a new treatment with a school, evidence-based practitioners should communicate that the pur-pose of the treatment is to help students meet educational goals and objectives as identified on the individualized education plan. Lastly, leader clients must also know how a treatment selection decision for one client can influence the other clients or students. When interven-tions clearly help many students learn or support most clients in meet-ing their behavioral goals, organizational leaders are more likely to risk the resources needed and manage the challenges that will emerge in order to adopt a new treatment for their system.

Professional Judgment

Professional judgment (sometimes called clinical expertise) is one of the most important aspects of evidence-based practice (EBP). Evidence-based practitioners use professional judgment to combine target client variables (e.g., needs, preferences) and stakeholder/leader client variables with evidence of treatment effectiveness in order to select the best intervention for a given client (Drisko & Grady, 2015). Good professional judgment is based on accessing all relevant information about the best available evidence and the clients (target/stakeholder/leader) as well as the context, so the best clinical decision is made. Professional judgment is essential throughout each step of the EBP process—which includes information gathering, treatment selection, data collection, and decisions to retain, adapt, or reject a treatment.

As was discussed in Section II, Best Available Evidence, identifying the best available evidence is not simply a matter of plucking a treatment off of a list of approved "effective" treatments. Good professional judgment involves being able to evaluate the literature and weigh the relevant forms of evidence that should influence treatment selection. Knowing about treatment evidence requires not only knowing which interventions research supports but also knowing the benefits and risks. The safety of using the procedure for everyone involved should enter the treatment selection process (Drisko & Grady, 2015).

Weighing different forms of evidence involves recognizing when the available literature deviates in meaningful ways from the situation a target client is currently experiencing.

When evidence-based practitioners lead the process of selecting treatments, they combine different forms of evidence for each viable treatment option with variables that are relevant to target, stakeholder, and leader clients. As was discussed in Section III, Target, Stakeholder, and Leader Clients, relevant target client variables include their health, the skills within their repertoire, their preferences, and the acceptability of the treatment options. For stakeholder clients, evidence-based practitioners will want to assess and integrate treatment acceptability and feasibility in terms of resource constraints, environmental supports, and capacity to implement a treatment with fidelity. For leader–stakeholder clients, variables relevant to systemic demands such as resources, staffing, and sustainability must be weighted and integrated into treatment selection. The evidence-based practice guide found in Appendix A can support evidence-based practitioners as they weigh and integrate these diverse sources of evidence and information.

Evidence-based practitioners cannot use sound professional judgment without relying on useful data. Target client behavior must improve and the only way to be certain this is the case is to have high-quality data. This is true even if the treatment that is implemented is identified as effective based on a systematic review and is the preferred intervention for all target, stakeholder, and leader clients. Chapter 10, Initial Selection: Weighing and Integrating Information, focuses on progress monitoring, because timely data collection that usefully informs the decision to retain, adapt, or reject a treatment is essential to the EBP decision-making process. Target client progress is necessary but insufficient for EBP to be fully realized. Data should be collected on tolerability and consumer satisfactions. Just as data should be regularly collected on target client goals, these target, stakeholder, and leader client data must be collected frequently to allow evidence-based practitioners to continue making decisions to retain, adapt, or reject treatments based on all relevant data.

CHAPTER 10

Initial Selection: Weighing and Integrating Information

Evidence-based practitioners must weigh relevant evidence as well as target/stakeholder/leader client information for every client they serve. There is no universal method for evaluating this information, but this chapter focuses on a process that evidence-based practitioners can use to weigh and integrate all relevant information so that the best treatment can be selected. If evidence-based practitioners ask all of these questions and follow their ethical guidelines, they will almost certainly be engaging in evidence-based practice (EBP) in a way that meets their clients' needs. This process will result in initial treatment selection and the effectiveness of the intervention must then be evaluated (see chapter: Progress Monitoring).

BEGINNING THE PROCESS OF EBP

As was described in the first section of this practitioner's guide, EBP should begin with the practical question that needs to be answered for each client (Spencer, Detrich, & Slocum, 2012). For example, the practical question could be, "How can we help a 20-year-old man develop skills so he can get a job?" or "How can we reduce a 9-year-old student's level of aggression, so we can avoid putting her in a more restrictive environment?" When evidence-based practitioners lose sight of the practical problem that initiated the EBP process, they are likely to select treatments that will not produce the best outcomes. Be sure to use the evidence-based practice guide from Appendix A as you review these steps.

Step 1: Identify the Best Source(s) of Evidence

Treatments are only selected in relation to the practical question being asked. Evidence-based practitioners are guided by the best source of evidence that most closely approximates the current situation. They examine the results from a credible systematic review. Whether or not a systematic review is credible is determined based on the information

A Practical Guide to Finding Treatments That Work for People with Autism.
DOI: http://dx.doi.org/10.1016/B978-0-12-809480-8.00010-8

provided in Chapter 1, Systematic Review (e.g., quality, quantity, consistency of outcomes, types of studies included in analyses, treatment categorization, etc.). Evidence-based practitioners ensure that the systematic review is relevant for the target client (e.g., diagnosis, age, etc.) and that it represents relatively recent work. If the systematic review was based on older studies, the evidence-based practitioner looks for other sources of information or seeks more information than is available in the older review. This process should result in a list of treatments that have been shown to be effective. If a treatment has been proposed for the client that does not appear on the list of effective treatments, evidence-based practitioners should examine whether it is consistent with the scientific principles of human behavior. Those treatments that are inconsistent with these principles should be deprioritized but should not necessarily be eliminated. Those treatments which are not behavioral in orientation but which may be effective should be conceptually analyzed by the evidence-based practitioner in terms of how and why they might be effective (i.e., what motivating operations, discriminative stimuli, and sources of reinforcement and extinction the procedures might consist of that could conceivably be effective; Brodhead, 2015).

Evidence-based practitioners will next examine client history and any current data that are available. Client history may be helpful in prioritizing the treatments remaining on the list. However, evidence-based practitioners should remember that client history should not be overinterpreted. For example, a treatment may not be effective because it was not implemented with fidelity or the target client may have acquired new skills that alter the likelihood the treatment could work at this point. In addition, recent data can help identify the best treatment from among the treatments options remaining. For example, if a functional analysis identified the function of behavior, an evidence-based practitioner would prioritize function-based treatments that are appropriate for the target client. Once all of these variables have been considered, the evidence-based practitioner constructs a list of "best" treatments that are rank ordered (prioritized) based on all sources of evidence. Evidence-based practitioners should base their decision on the best available evidence—but that is not the same thing as saying that they should only pay attention when there is a *lot* of evidence that is of the *highest* quality/relevance (Slocum, Detrich, & Spencer, 2012). Science does not consistently offer us such easy choices. For example, a systematic review on autism treatments for adults does not show a lot of treatment options to be effective with this age group. In fact, the only treatment identified as effective according to the NSP 2.0 (National Autism Center, 2015) was "behavioral interventions." However the evidence-based practitioner needing to address communication skills would prioritize treatments that have "emerging" evidence (e.g., functional communication training), are conceptually consistent with the science of human behavior, and which research shows have been effective with similar populations (e.g., adults with other developmental or intellectual disabilities).

Step 2: Review Relevant Target Client Variables That Could Impact Treatment Selection

Evidence-based practitioners next prioritize those treatments remaining on their list based on client variables (health, repertoire, preference, and social validity). Medications, medical conditions, comorbidity, biological variables (e.g., hormones), or mental health issues may all explain target behaviors or influence whether or not a treatment is a good fit for a client. The treatments being considered should be reprioritized based on this information.

Evidence-based practitioners also prioritize treatments based on the target client's repertoire. They assess if the client has the prerequisite skills needed for the treatment to be effective. If the client lacks the prerequisite skills, the treatment should not be considered at this time. However, it is worth having a conversation with the stakeholder clients about the intervention. They may choose to build the prerequisite skill, so it is an option in the future. In addition, although it is certainly not always possible, if one of the treatments on the list of effective interventions could result in a behavioral cusp (i.e., a behavior change that leads to new opportunities, reinforcers, etc.), that treatment should be given a higher priority.

Evidence-based practitioners place considerable weight on client preferences, as discussed in Chapter 5, Client Preferences. Treatments that use results of a developmentally appropriate preference assessment to develop a consequence-based intervention should be given a higher priority. But there is vast literature on choice, so evidence-based practitioners should be familiar with this literature and use choice when appropriate. Similarly, there are treatment options that provide more opportunity for preference (e.g., environmental enrichment, contingency contracting). Treatments should be prioritized if preference is a natural by-product of the intervention.

Social validity should be a primary concern for evidence-based practitioners. Evidence-based practitioners provide services to clients to improve their quality of life. Treatments that (1) expand life opportunities, (2) help clients connect with the people who are important to them and their communities, and (3) more closely resemble the experiences of the rest of population while offering the life experiences the client wants should be given a higher priority. In addition, higher priority should be given to treatments that are likely to lead to generalization of skills across relevant and real-world situations and are acceptable to the client. Treatments that risk the physical and social well-being of clients should be deprioritized and ideally, eliminated.

Step 3: Review Relevant Stakeholder and Leader Client Variables That Impact Treatment Selection

With the reprioritized list in hand, evidence-based practitioners consider the values, preferences, and real-world challenges faced by stakeholder and leader clients. For example, information about family quality of life should be evaluated in relation to all treatment options being considered. The feasibility of treatment should be used to reprioritize the list further. In addition to monetary resources, there are often a range of environmental supports that must be present in order for a treatment to be effective. The absence of environmental supports may mean a treatment could not possibly work, even if there is a lot of evidence to support its use and it is highly preferred by all parties. Inability to attain treatment fidelity is an indicator that a treatment may not be feasible. If stakeholder clients cannot implement the intervention accurately once provided appropriate training and coaching, the treatment may simply not be feasible. Finally, even if stakeholder clients are able to implement a treatment with fidelity, if they are unable to sustain that level of fidelity for the entire period that the intervention must be implemented to produce needed change, the treatment should be deprioritized.

Evidence-based practitioners connect with leader clients and identify the range of issues that these decision-makers believe should impact treatment selection (e.g., staff experience, resource reallocation, impact on target client and other clients, match with cultural norms, etc.).

Once this broad range of social validity, feasibility, and sustainability data have been gathered from stakeholder and leader clients, the evidence-based practitioner reprioritizes the treatments again.

Step 4: Identify Short- and Long-Term Goals

Evidence-based practitioners facilitate a conversation among target, stakeholder, and leader clients to discuss the treatment options and why each intervention is given a higher or lower priority. They actively encourage these clients to discuss their concerns and strategies for overcoming barriers for preferred treatments. It is only at this point that an initial treatment selection is made. Ideally, this initial treatment is effective and no further modifications will be needed. Unfortunately, this will not always be the case. Determining how to proceed after behavior or skills have not improved is discussed in Chapter 11, Progress Monitoring and Chapter 12, Determining the Next Step.

The process of initially selecting the treatment may be very simple or it may result from a challenging discussion filled with very different (and sometimes opposing) views. The evidence-based practitioner can facilitate a smoother discussion by knowing all concerns and understanding the organizational culture prior to the initial treatment selection meeting.

Some treatments are a very small departure from the interventions already in place, so complexity will not play as central a part in the discussion. Sometimes the initial treatment selection decision involves implementing more than one treatment (e.g., modeling and token economy). Evidence-based practitioners discuss the unique challenges of implementing more than one treatment simultaneously (e.g., increase in resources and environmental supports). On some occasions, more than one treatment is appropriate but the team (the evidence-based practitioner, stakeholder and leader clients, and target client, when appropriate) may determine that these treatments will be phased in so they can be implemented with fidelity. Using this partnership-based model of intervention is more likely to increase acceptability, contextual fit, and treatment fidelity (Sanetti, Chafouleas, Fallon, & Jaffrey, 2014).

When appropriate, evidence-based practitioners suggest the possibility of identifying both short- and long-term treatments. For example, a school system might agree that a given treatment (e.g., a community-school Job Skills program for adolescents) should be implemented, but the challenges with resource reallocation and scheduling training means the target client could not access the intervention in the near future. Currently, multiple effective strategies can be implemented with a high degree of fidelity (e.g., use of task analysis with prompting and reinforcement for job skills plus modeling). The evidence-based practitioner helps the team to select both treatments. The short-term treatment can be implemented with fidelity, but a clear implementation plan is devised to develop the capacity to implement the more complex intervention (i.e., the community-school Job Skills program). Realistic discussions about the training/coaching that will be needed to implement the intervention with fidelity must occur.

Irrespective of whether an intervention is a short- or a long-term treatment, implementation planning is necessary (see appendix: Sample Implementation Plan Checklist). Implementation planning serves the purpose of individualizing and adapting a treatment based on the context (Collier-Meek, Sanetti, & Boyle, 2015). Action and coping planning are both critical to implementation planning. When action planning, the evidence-based practitioner and stakeholder clients review all steps needed to implement the intervention and adapt the treatment so that it fits the context. It is at this point that all resource constraints and environmental supports are reconsidered so that reasonable adaptations to the intervention can be made. Adaptations are published in the literature and they are a necessary component of EBP because real-world situations never perfectly mirror research conditions. However, evidence-based practitioners should maximize the similarity of the adapted intervention to the treatment procedures identified in the scientific literature. Evidence-based practitioners review the adapted protocol and compare it against the literature or resources that identify critical components of interventions. For example, the National Professional Development Center on Autism Spectrum Disorder has provided extensive resources at http://autismpdc.fpg.unc.edu/evidence-based-practices. Adaptations should be reviewed to determine if they violate the scientific principles of human behavior. Action planning also involves (1) determining when each step will be implemented, (2) establishing how often the step will be implemented, and (3) finalizing how long each treatment step will be implemented.

Coping planning is the second component of implementation planning and involves identifying potential barriers to implementation and problem-solving around each barrier. This is an ongoing part of the EBP process. That is, coping planning should continue throughout intervention implementation and should result from the collection of new evidence.

IMPLEMENT AND REVIEW TREATMENT

Implementation planning also involves measuring treatment fidelity, the quality of adherence to treatment protocols, and whether or not the intervention was implemented as planned (Collier-Meek et al., 2015). Each of these variables will be briefly addressed in Chapter 11, Progress Monitoring. These steps are critical to the EBP decision-making model. Once treatment implementation begins, the evidence-based practitioner collects and uses new sources of evidence.

Step 5: Review New Evidence

Evidence-based practitioners collect data that allow the team to make decisions about whether or not the intervention is working. The data collection technique should match the practical question that is being asked. Procedures for determining the best type of data to collect are comprehensively outlined in books dedicated to this topic (e.g., Kazdin, 2011). However the appropriateness of a given data collection is also based on who is collecting the data and their experience with data collection. Issues relevant to data collection are briefly discussed further in Chapter 11, Progress Monitoring.

Evidence-based practitioners collect data on treatment fidelity, quality of adherence, and the extent to which the treatment has been implemented as planned. Treatment fidelity data are essential both for determining if the treatment is feasible and if the target client is actually accessing the treatment. A treatment that is not being accurately implemented should not be rejected unless the team determines it is not feasible. First, the evidence-based practitioner must facilitate a problem-solving discussion to overcome obstacles. Even highly qualified professionals can follow the steps of a protocol but miss an important component, so the quality of implementation should be evaluated. The steps of a treatment can be technically implemented, but an essential aspect of one or more of the steps may not be sufficient. This is addressed in more detail in Chapter 11, Progress Monitoring. Evidence-based practitioners compare when the intervention was implemented in relation to the proposed schedule in the implementation plan. It is also important to identify barriers that prevent scheduled implementation and determine if these barriers have been adequately addressed.

Several forms of evidence will need to be collected on an ongoing basis once the treatment is implemented. For example, client preference should be assessed again after the treatment has been initiated. In addition, evidence-based practitioners assess the tolerability of the treatment. That is, can the target client tolerate the treatment as indicated by positive or negative enthusiasm or affect. Consumer satisfaction data are collected from the target, stakeholder, and leader clients. Through intervention implementation, these consumers may determine that they find a treatment unacceptable or that unanticipated barriers to treatment fidelity make the intervention unfeasible. Evidence-based practitioners continue supporting the team based on ongoing data collection as further determinations about the treatment are made.

Step 6: Determine Next Steps

Once the evidence-based practitioner has reviewed the new evidence that is generated from intervention implementation, they facilitate a discussion that determines what steps should be taken next. There are three options. First, the treatment might be retained as it is, but a plan for eventually fading the treatment is developed. Second, the treatment may need to be adapted. Evidence-based practitioners advocate for the smallest adaptation necessary to address the area(s) of concern. They assess if the adaptations violate the principles upon which the treatment is implemented and ensure that critical components of treatment are not being removed (or weakened to the extent that the intervention will not work). Third, the treatment may be rejected when (1) a client is not making progress, (2) progress occurs at a pace that is too slow to be meaningful, (3) meaningful gains are not being made, (4) the treatment cannot be implemented with fidelity, or (5) resource/environmental supports have changed resulting in a lack of sustainability for the intervention. When this occurs, the evidence-based practitioner returns to Step 1 of the EBP guide armed with new information. The selection of an alternate treatment usually occurs quickly because the team has already completely the process previously. This process is described in more detail in Chapter 11, Progress Monitoring.

Progress Monitoring

Progress monitoring is the best source of evidence once a treatment has been implemented (Slocum, Detrich, & Spencer, 2012). Progress monitoring involves collecting data for the purpose of making timely and accurate decisions about treatment effectiveness. There are two primary variables that need to be completed for proper progress monitoring to occur. To begin, high-quality data must be collected frequently enough that evidence-based practitioners can make speedy decisions about treatment effectiveness. Ethical evidence-based practitioners use treatments that are effective and shift to alternate treatments when it is clear that the treatment initially selected is not working. It is not always easy to determine that a treatment will not be effective. Evidence-based practitioners need to use their professional judgment to determine how long a treatment should take to produce a meaningful change. Learning occurs more rapidly for some clients than others, for a variety of reasons. For example, a gifted client with ASD will generally respond more quickly to the same treatment than a client with ASD who has comorbid intellectual disability due to the capacity to rapidly identify changing environmental conditions. In addition to high-quality data, evidence-based practitioners must be able to interpret the data and support the stakeholder clients (and when appropriate target clients) in drawing data-based conclusions about treatment effectiveness. This means evidence-based practitioners must appropriately use single-subject research design (SSRD) in a way that clearly answers the practical question, but are efficient for the stakeholder clients and context. Both data collection methods and SSRD are addressed below.

DATA COLLECTION

Identifying the Correct Data Collectxion Method

Entire books are dedicated to data collection and SSRD, so a comprehensive analysis of these topics is beyond the scope of this practitioner's guide. A cursory review of these topics follows.

A Practical Guide to Finding Treatments That Work for People with Autism.
DOI: http://dx.doi.org/10.1016/B978-0-12-809480-8.00011-X

What Kind of Data Collection System Should I Use?

Continuous measurement occurs when *all* instances of behavior are detected and recorded, such as frequency/event or duration data. Capturing all data is preferable to only a portion of the data so that precise levels of problem behaviors or skills are represented. However, continuous data collection is not always feasible given resource constraints or environmental supports. Discontinuous measurement occurs when samples of the behavior or skills of interest are detected and recorded. Examples include interval sampling (e.g., whole interval, partial interval) and momentary time sampling. A final common method of data collection involves the use of permanent products. Permanent products represent the collection of real or concrete objects that reflect demonstration of behavior or use of skills in naturally occurring activities. For example, to assess if a spelling intervention was effective, performance on the weekly spelling test could serve as the data, with percentage of correct responses being the indicator of improvement. Evidence-based practitioners are encouraged to reference books or other resources that discuss data collection methods and SSRD (e.g., Kazdin, 2011).

How Frequently Should I Collect Data?

Evidence-based practitioners make decisions on the basis of multiple data points. Data should be collected at the most frequent schedule possible, as determined with the stakeholder and leader clients. It is very difficult to make timely decisions if data are collected less than once a week because it would take more than a month before an analysis of intervention effectiveness could occur. More frequent data collection is advisable so that treatment effectiveness can more efficiently be made. This will be particularly critical when the consequences of having an ineffective treatment in place are most significant (e.g., the target client is injuring himself or others, decisions about the restrictiveness of environment are being considered, etc.). In addition, very frequent data collection is necessary when the implemented treatment is based on lower quality evidence (e.g., other than a systematic review) or has been ineffectively used in the past.

How Do I Know If the Data Are Credible?

Interobserver agreement (IOA) reflects the degree to which two observers agree about the occurrence or non-occurrence of a target behavior. Obtaining high IOA begins with generating good operational definitions and then training two or more data collectors until they can consistently rate the same level of the behavior/skill that is being observed. In practice, professionals often do not collect IOA data due to resource constraints or a lack of environmental supports. However, IOA data should be collected at least a portion of the time an intervention is being implemented because a single data collector will likely "drift" away from the correct interpretation of the definition over time. The result is that the evidence-based practitioner will report that a treatment is effective when it is actually ineffective (or vice versa). Typically, IOA of 80% or greater is necessary to produce believable data. When this level of IOA cannot be achieved, the data collection system may be too complex for the data collectors and/or the context. Alternative data collection procedures may be needed.

Final Procedural Issues in Data Collection
Evidence-based practitioners collect data to ensure that the treatment remains effective even after the passage of time (i.e., maintenance data). In addition, evidence-based practitioners collect generalization data to show that the skill or behavior is being demonstrated across relevant settings, with all stakeholder clients, or when different materials are used, etc. These data help demonstrate the social validity of the intervention.

Single-Subject Research Design
SSRD should be used by all evidence-based practitioners, irrespective of their field of specialization. Collecting data without being able to interpret the outcomes in a meaningful and accurate manner merely wastes resources and unnecessarily saps needed supports in the treatment environment. Evidence-based practitioners are encouraged to use books and online resources (e.g., https://foxylearning.com/tutorials/va) that will review their previous training on SSRD. Although a comprehensive discussion of SSRD is not possible in this practitioner's guide, a list of commonly used SSRDs is provided in Table 11.1.

Evidence-based practitioners should discuss each research design in a pragmatic way with stakeholder clients. The purpose of using SSRD (i.e., understanding whether or not a treatment works) is best explained when it is tied to the real concerns facing stakeholder and leader clients. For example, ABAB or withdrawal designs will be viewed as more acceptable when the goal is to determine if the intervention is still

Table 11.1 Single-Subject Research Designs		
Single-Subject Research Design	Definition	Strengths and Limitations
AB Design	• A research design consisting of a baseline and a single intervention condition	• Simplest design but does not allow evidence-based practitioner to draw firm conclusions about treatment effectiveness
Alternating Treatments Design	• A research design in which two or more treatments conditions are alternated repeatedly	• Allows the evidence-based practitioner to compare two or more treatments but much care must be taken to avoid carryover effects and treatment fidelity with two treatments may be challenging in real-world settings
Multiple Baseline	• A research design in which baseline data are collected and treatment is applied in one setting, with one participant, or to one behavior and withheld from other settings, participants, and behaviors until it can be systematically introduced to control for chance changes in responding	• Allows the evidence-based practitioner to avoid ABAB design and collect data across relevant settings, clients, or behaviors/skills, but because the introduction of treatments is staggered, some settings, clients, or behaviors/skills may wait a long time before intervention is accessed
ABAB	• A research design consisting of a repeated series of baseline and intervention conditions	• Simple but requires withdrawal of the treatment, which is often objectionable to stakeholder clients and is unethical under a limited number of conditions
Changing Criterion	• A research design consisting of graduated steps from baseline to a predetermined goal involving systematic changes in criterion levels of performance	• Allows the evidence-based practitioner to gradually increase the expectation for the client but magnitude of criterion changes and pace of change may be challenging for stakeholder clients

necessary (Elliott, 1988). In addition, helping stakeholder clients to understand what the data mean will help them decide to invest the extra effort required. Stakeholder clients will have a difficult time understanding the value of both data collection and SSRD if they do not have at least a rudimentary understanding of the magnitude of change, steady state, the need for multiple data points, and a functional relationship. These terms can be overwhelming, so evidence-based practitioners should take the time to explain them in everyday terms (e.g., "We need to know whether the treatment really made the behavior decrease," rather than "We need to determine whether there is a functional relationship between the intervention and behavior").

Additional Sources of Data
Treatment Fidelity

Treatment fidelity is not something that should be established just once. Evidence-based practitioners should make sure that implementation does not deviate across time (Bellg et al., 2004). Scholars have not yet established what level of treatment fidelity is necessary to produce needed changes for target clients. It is likely that the level of fidelity needed will be different for different treatments and different clients. Borelli et al. (2005) used a criterion of 80% for a review of the literature because they assumed this was a reasonably high level of fidelity. However, this decision was not data based, it was based on reason. In some cases, fidelity may drop below 80% and still produce change. In many other cases, treatment fidelity must be higher than 80% to produce meaningful changes for the target client behavior. "How do evidence-based practitioners proceed given there is no evidence-based standard for treatment fidelity?" Evidence-based practitioners collect treatment fidelity data and data on target client progress before making individualized decisions based on these data. If the target client is not making progress on the skill or behavior, it may be that treatment fidelity is too low and that additional training and/or coaching will be needed to improve the consistency and accuracy of intervention implementation. That may be true even when treatment fidelity data are at a level of 80% or greater. But if treatment fidelity is reasonably high and progress is not being made, it may indicate that the intervention, as designed, is not feasible and/or effective. Evidence-based practitioners need to use both data and sound professional judgment to determine the best course of action.

Quality of Adherence

Quality of adherence refers to the extent to which the essential characteristics of the treatment are implemented. A personal example clarifies quality of adherence. My staff once told me a treatment no longer worked for a client (let's call him Timmy), and they wanted to move to a more complex intervention that would require a lot of resources. I reviewed the treatment fidelity data, which were very good (over 90%), and then decided to observe the session myself. After observing for a few minutes, I asked to step in and work with Timmy myself. To the shock of my staff, Timmy immediately responded to the intervention. The protocol required delivering verbal praise. The staff consistently said, "Good job," but that was part of the problem.

They used a monotone voice when saying "Good job" every time Timmy was right. I was excited to see Timmy do well so I said, "Way to go, Timmy!" or "You are so awesome at this, my man!" I also modulated the tone of my voice (Timmy preferred a quiet enthusiasm). The staff had been delivering verbal praise, but it did not serve as a reinforcer. With very simple training of staff, Timmy made progress when working with everyone. Quality of adherence data can be collected simultaneously with treatment fidelity data, so this may be the most efficient data collection system evidence-based practitioners can use.

Implementation Plan
Evidence-based practitioners compare the implementation plan (i.e., an outline of every step that must be completed so that a treatment can be accurately implemented) against what happened in reality. When evidence-based practitioners work closely with stakeholder and leader clients to develop an implementation plan and there are significant differences between what was planned and what occurred, it may indicate that the treatment is not feasible and a different treatment should be considered. Alternately, the implementation plan may serve as a source for discussing barriers and brainstorming about how to resolve these problems.

Target Client Preference and Tolerability
Consideration of target client preference should not be restricted to initial treatment selection. Data should be collected on preference during the treatment implementation phase. In the fields of health, medication (Liu et al., 2016) and other medical interventions (Aparicio et al., 2016) tolerability (or tolerance) following treatment implementation are assessed. Tolerability represents the extent to which adverse effects are endured by the patient. With educational and behavioral interventions, tolerability can be assessed following treatment implementation by examining affect and enthusiasm. This indicates both preference for a treatment and tolerability of the intervention. Affect and enthusiasm will be particularly useful indicators of target client preference and tolerability when communication skills are extremely limited. Affect and enthusiasm have been measured in children with ASD who are receiving therapeutic services since the 1970s (Koegel & Egel, 1979; Koegel, Werner, Vismara, & Koegel, 2005). Occurrence of positive affect can be measured even in very young children by examining smiling, laughing, and physical affection (hugging and kissing; Vernon, Koegel,

Dauterman, & Stolen, 2012). Affect and enthusiasm can also be measured on other dimensions. For example, negative enthusiasm (e.g., attempts to leave the room, pushes the task away, etc.), neutral enthusiasm (e.g., fidgety, moments of inattention, etc.), and positive enthusiasm (e.g., performs task and attends to stimulus materials; laughs or smiles while working) may be useful ways of measuring preference for or intolerance of a treatment. Children, adolescents, and adults with ASD will express many of these reactions to therapeutic conditions and these observable and measurable behaviors should be included in the data collection process. Although these data by themselves may not force the rejection of a treatment, evidence-based practitioners should discuss these data when determining whether to retain, adapt, or reject a treatment. A treatment associated with slow progress and high levels of negative affect/enthusiasm might need to be adapted or rejected (see Chapter 12). In addition, if two or more treatments are likely to be of similar effectiveness, then the one that produces more positive affect for the client should be prioritized.

Target Client Satisfaction
Consumer satisfaction data have been collected in research involving children (Lopata, Thomeer, et al., 2015), adolescents (White et al., 2013), and adults with ASD (Turner-Brown, Perry, Dichter, Bodfish, & Penn, 2008). These data are typically collected at the end of research studies, but this is not always the case. For example, Pugliese and White (2014) collected data after every therapeutic session when they worked with college students with ASD. They asked questions such as: "How helpful was the session?," "How helpful was the homework?," "Did you learn anything in the session?," "Which components of training within session are helpful or unhelpful?," "And did they continue to use the strategies after treatment was concluded?"

Adolescents with ASD have provided consumer satisfaction data by evaluating the treatment as a whole and rank-ordering treatment components based on their helpfulness (White et al., 2013). This approach can be particularly helpful in getting target clients to disclose which aspects of treatments they find dissatisfying. Evidence-based practitioners then query further to understand how they can create a more useful treatment protocol for the target client. Translating research into practice is not only critical at the treatment level but also with respect to collecting and meaningfully using consumer satisfaction data. Most researchers generate their own consumer satisfaction data that are geared specifically to the objectives of the study. Evidence-based practitioners should do the same. That is, the consumer satisfaction data they collect should be somewhat individualized based on the goals of treatment (although some overlap across clients will be likely).

Attrition and nonattendance may also indicate a problem with consumer satisfaction, treatment acceptability, and treatment feasibility (Koenig et al., 2010; Pahnke, Lundgren, Hursti, & Hirvikoski, 2013). When target clients drop out of treatment altogether (attrition) or skip scheduled sessions (nonattendance), it may indicate they are dissatisfied with treatment (or the therapist). However, evidence-based practitioners do not assume consumer satisfaction is high simply because a target client continues using their services. Target clients and relevant stakeholders may not be able to access similar services elsewhere due to a limited number of practitioners in a region or because the other practitioners have long waiting lists. Nonattendance is worrisome for multiple reasons. Nonattendance is important not only for financial reasons (i.e., no services can be billed during that time period) but also because continuity of service is important for achieving therapeutic goals, particularly for people with ASD. Whenever target clients skip sessions, evidence-based practitioners should assess why nonattendance has occurred. It is important to remember that clients may seek to please therapists and may not easily share the reasons behind nonattendance. Evidence-based practitioners should reinforce the sharing of any concerns for all types of clients. Even when client concerns pose an unexpected challenge or barrier (e.g., they are not happy with the way the practitioner interacts with them), clients should be reassured that their concerns are being taken seriously. Every effort should be made to resolve the concern.

Stakeholder Client Satisfaction
Evidence-based practitioners also assess consumer satisfaction with stakeholder clients. Like target client satisfaction data, stakeholder client satisfaction has significant implications for the feasibility, usefulness, and quality of treatment. This may include parents, teachers, and staff who provide direct services to individuals with ASD. Parents are stakeholder clients even if they do not provide direct services to their children. Lopata, Thomeer, et al. (2015) provide examples on how to collect stakeholder satisfaction data that are unique to the specific

treatment being implemented and the role the stakeholder holds. For example, parents rated:

- staff understanding of child needs,
- child progress,
- enjoyment,
- cooperation and communication,
- services,
- parenting classes,
- effectiveness of treatment,
- overall satisfaction,
- comparison with other programs.

In contrast, staff rated satisfaction on the following dimensions:

- Clarity of duties
- Utility of required readings and manual
- Effectiveness of training
- Effectiveness of feedback in increasing performance
- Timeliness of supervisor responses
- Recommendation of the position to others

Asking open-ended questions allows stakeholder clients to identify areas of strength or concern that were not easily anticipated (Turner-Brown et al., 2008). The evidence-based practitioner should also return to the practical problem when assessing stakeholder client satisfaction. For example, they should ask, "When we first met, you were concerned with (fill in the blank). How has that been going recently?" (adapted from The Research Units on Paediatric Psychopharmacology and Psychosocial Interventions (RUPP Autism Network; Arnold et al., 2003)). This sample of methods for collecting client satisfaction data from research has been offered because little information is available about client satisfaction in practice. That is, the extent to which client satisfaction data are collected and used in practice is not readily available. However, problems with client satisfaction can quickly undermine the goals of therapy, so it is essential.

Leader Client Satisfaction
Just as it is essential to assess client satisfaction among target and stakeholder clients, it is important to assess the leader client's satisfaction on an ongoing basis. As noted previously, there are a wide range

of systemic issues that may influence the leader client's views about the appropriateness of an intervention. Leader clients primarily make the decision to adopt a treatment, particularly when there are systemic implications for the adoption of the treatment (Strain, Barton, & Dunlap, 2012). For this reason, evidence-based practitioners would be wise to assess leader client's views about the systemic impact once an intervention has been implemented. Whenever leader clients have been involved in the treatment selection process, their level of satisfaction regarding a treatment should be evaluated—even when their involvement has been very limited. Leader clients may make decisions regarding the continued feasibility of the intervention in the current case, the use or reallocation of resources required for treatment implementation on an ongoing basis, or the utility of adopting the treatment at a systemic level. Understanding and making decisions based on leader client satisfaction may be particularly critical for resource-/support-intensive interventions or those that require the involvement of a large number of the organizational community (e.g., peer training). Like target and stakeholder consumer satisfaction data, evidence-based practitioners should make decisions about the continued use of an intervention based on these data.

Using Client Satisfaction Data
Evidence-based practitioners know that the environment they create will directly influence the behavior of all clients (target, stakeholder, and leaders). To maximize outcomes, evidence-based practitioners collect and use these data to make changes when satisfaction is insufficient. A treatment may be rejected based on client satisfaction data even when it has produced the desired behavior change. For example, a client who has increased rates of social interaction during social skills training may be dissatisfied with the treatment because he feels stigmatized by attending the group and has started drinking alcohol to manage his distress. Alternative options for increasing social skills training should be considered—even though improvements have been noted. Similarly, the evidence-based practitioner serving a target client who finds a treatment intolerable can adapt a treatment in many ways. For example:

• Assess and alter the task difficulty. A plan to gradually increase task difficulty when negative enthusiasm decreases should be developed.

- Strengthen the schedule of reinforcement until positive enthusiasm and affect increase.
- Identify and use more potent reinforcers until positive enthusiasm and affect increase.

Stakeholder client satisfaction should influence treatment decisions because dissatisfaction is meaningful to the stakeholder client, and it has direct bearing on the likelihood that the target client outcomes will be actualized. For example, behavioral contrast (an improvement in performance in one setting that has a corresponding worsening in another setting) may result in parental dissatisfaction with treatment despite the fact the target client's behavior is improving during treatment sessions. It is easy to focus exclusively on the progress monitoring data that show client improvement in the treatment settings, but evidence-based practitioners recognize that this phenomenon has resulted in a very real problem faced by stakeholder clients (i.e., the family). They can resolve this concern by strengthening the schedule of reinforcement across settings so that generalization of treatment outcomes results (Koegel, Egel, & Williams, 1980). In this case the evidence-based practitioner can simultaneously increase parental satisfaction and improve target client behavior across environments by using this information. But this outcome will not be realized unless evidence-based practitioners have created an environment in which target, stakeholder, and leader clients have the opportunity to share dissatisfaction and doing so results in favorable outcomes. That is, evidence-based practitioners sustain a history of responding to client concerns.

Leader client satisfaction data should also be collected and should impact decision-making. For example, a treatment may have been selected because it was effective, matched identified needs based on client variables, and was deemed feasible and/or socially valid by all parties. However, once the treatment was implemented, it became apparent that more resources would be required and the time needed before staff could be trained to the criterion was not reasonable. Functionally the client was not accessing an effective intervention because it could not be accurately implemented. Similarly, the resources that would be required would take considerable time to obtain (e.g., a grant would need to be secured). For these client- and system-level concerns, the leader client may report a higher degree of dissatisfaction. In this case the proposed implementation plan is not working. The current implementation plan may be shifted to a long-term treatment plan and alternate treatments options may be reconsidered as the short-term treatment solution.

CONFLICTING FORMS OF EVIDENCE

The greatest challenge evidence-based practitioners can face is when target client outcome data show that a client's behavior or skills are improving but target, stakeholder, and/or leader client consumer satisfaction data suggest that there is a significant problem with ongoing implementation. There is no absolute correct decision in this case. First, a different treatment could be implemented. The alternate treatment that is approved by all stakeholders could also alter behavior in a powerful and meaningful way and result in a favorable outcome. Unfortunately a different treatment may not produce favorable outcomes. Only data will clarify. Second, target, stakeholder, and/or leader clients may be dissatisfied with the treatment but may find it tolerable if it addresses the practical problem being addressed, particularly if target client behavior/skill improvement is occurring rapidly/steadily and the treatment can be faded quickly. Third, target, stakeholder, and/or leader client dissatisfaction might be reduced to a neutral or acceptable level if the evidence-based practitioner facilitates a brainstorming session and areas of concern can be resolved. This strategy will be most successful when the resources and supports required for alternative options are deemed impractical or unacceptable.

CHAPTER 12

Determining the Next Step

RETAINING TREATMENTS: A PLAN TO FADE INTERVENTIONS

As described previously, evidence-based practitioners weigh and integrate different forms of evidence to select treatments. Ongoing data collection helps evidence-based practitioners weigh and integrate new sources of information in order to make decisions about retaining, adapting, or rejecting treatments. Ideally, treatments are retained because they are considered acceptable/feasible and they produce socially important improvements for the target client that results in meaningful gains in quality of life. Even when this is the case, the evidence-based practitioners work is not done. Evidence-based practitioners generate a plan to fade the intervention based on the trajectory of the data. That is, treatments can be faded more quickly when improvements have been achieved and sustained. As always, the evidence-based practitioner works with target, stakeholder, and leader clients to devise a realistic plan for fading the treatment. The fading plan should also include the level of change in a target client's behavior that would trigger a return to intervention implementation if ongoing success is not sustained. For example, a plan to thin a schedule of reinforcement or the frequency with which a Social Story™ is read might be in place. However the target client's behavior shifts below criterion once the treatment has been faded. Performance is either consistently below the criterion or is inconsistent (sometimes above and sometimes below the criterion). This should trigger a plan to resume the previous dosage of intervention and a new (more gradual) plan to fade the intervention should be developed. Just as with all other treatment decisions, issues that are important to stakeholders should be incorporated into the decision-making process. For example, a parent may want to wait to fade the treatment until after a big family gathering in a few weeks or a teacher may want to fade the intervention immediately because only a month remains before the end of the school year, and he hopes to have a less intensive intervention in place before summer break.

A Practical Guide to Finding Treatments That Work for People with Autism.
DOI: http://dx.doi.org/10.1016/B978-0-12-809480-8.00012-1

ADAPTING TREATMENTS

A treatment may need to be adapted based on new evidence that is collected after an intervention is implemented. Evidence-based practitioners use their best professional judgment to make adaptations. They try to:

- minimize the size of the adaptation,
- ensure components critical to treatment effectiveness are retained, and
- determine if the adaptation violates the principles on which the treatment is based.

The smallest adaptation that produces positive target client outcomes but still addresses target, stakeholder, and leader client concerns should be made. Greater adaptations are likely to result in an additional need for resources and environmental support. Once the stakeholder client is trained to implement the treatment accurately, more significant adaptations to the treatment procedures can result in confusion, leading to a decrement in treatment fidelity. In addition, one of the primary reasons for selecting the treatment initially is because sufficient research supports its use. Greater deviations from the protocol used in research mean the intervention being implemented may no longer be supported by strong evidence. By making smaller adaptations, there is a lower likelihood that the components critical to treatment effectiveness will be eliminated. When adaptations are proposed, the changes should be evaluated to determine whether or not they violate the scientific principles on which the treatment is based. If a violation of scientific principles is proposed, alternative adaptations should be considered because the likelihood a treatment will be effective is much lower.

The evidence-based practitioner may enter a meeting with target, stakeholder, and/or leader clients with the plan to adapt a treatment but find that the modifications that are being proposed would result in an intervention that could not address the practical question that initiated the process. When this occurs, the evidence-based practitioner explains the concerns and proposes alternate modifications. If this process does not result in a treatment that is likely to be effective and acceptable to target, stakeholder, and/or leader clients, the evidence-based practitioner may instead propose that the treatment be rejected and other alternatives be considered. However, this decision should be made only if the evidence-based practitioner has an overwhelmingly compelling reason to believe the practical question cannot be addressed based on the proposed adaptations.

REJECTING TREATMENTS

The decision to reject a treatment is typically made when meaningful improvement in behavior or skills has not occurred. But a treatment may also be rejected when progress occurs at a rate that is too slow to be meaningful, when stakeholder and/or leader clients determine that the treatment requires too many resources or environmental supports, or treatment fidelity cannot be sustained at a high level in the real-world situations (e.g., treatment fidelity was high during training but not in the natural environment). Treatment rejection is a team decision. However the evidence-based practitioner must take care to ensure that the treatment is not being rejected too quickly. For example, a client with ASD who has a comorbid intellectual disability may not respond to treatment very quickly. If the treatment has been in place for a short period of time, progress may not be evidenced; however, improvements would occur if the treatment were sustained for a longer period of time. Similarly, a client may not make progress quickly when they have been ill, there are significant changes in their environment, or the treatment could not consistently be implemented with fidelity. All of the data need to be examined and integrated before the decision to reject a treatment is made. Once the decision to reject a treatment is made, the evidence-based practitioner returns to Step 1 of the EBP process and re-examines the new evidence. Selection of an alternate treatment should proceed quickly because the team members have all completed the process previously, understand the treatment options, and have access to all new information.

Conclusions and Examples

To use the evidence-based practice (EBP) decision-making process to select effective treatments that can be practically implemented in real-world settings, evidence-based practitioners use their professional judgment to integrate the best available evidence with target, stakeholder, and client needs and concerns. As described in this practitioner's guide, this process is complex and challenging to implement. As a result, evidence-based practitioners need to consistently work to have current knowledge about both the evidence that is available, the strengths and limitations of these sources of evidence, and the very real challenges faced by the clients (target, stakeholder, and leader) that are served.

TREATMENTS NOT IDENTIFIED AS EFFECTIVE

Although evidence-based practitioners promote treatments that have been demonstrated to be effective, other practitioners may not do so. Furthermore, stakeholder and leader clients are often highly motivated to use treatments that have little or no empirical support. Like the evidence-based practitioner, they are motivated to help a client with ASD to have a better quality of life. They sometimes have anecdotal evidence (e.g., the approach worked with their friend's daughter, it seemed to work with another student, etc.). Evidence-based practitioners are strongly encouraged to read an article by Brodhead (2015) about how to navigate this difficult challenge. Briefly, he recommends asking questions like, "Is the client's safety at risk?," "Could the treatment work if it were translated into behavioral principles?," "Could the implementation of the treatment negatively impact progress toward goal achievement?" Unless a treatment can hurt a child, could not possibly be effective based on scientific explanations of human behavior, and could significantly hurt the client with ASD, he suggests that the intervention should be considered as a potential solution. Evidence-based practitioners advocate for treatments that have strong evidence of effectiveness; however, alienation of stakeholder and leader clients can result in more dramatic challenges for the client than testing out an unproven treatment. Evidence-based practitioners can bring their skills in data collection and SSRD to the table and support the team when they select one of these alternate treatments. They will, however, voice their ethical concerns if they believe the treatment will do harm to the target client.

PLANNING TO IMPROVE EBP AT A LOCAL LEVEL

This brief section acknowledges a final challenge evidence-based practitioners seeking to engage in the process of EBP will likely face. Practitioners often receive insufficient training at universities to fully engage in the process of EBP (Drisko & Grady, 2015). This places a great responsibility on evidence-based practitioners to learn how to evaluate the literature in relation to the real-world contexts in which they work. It may be necessary to form a supportive group to examine the literature within a more local organization (e.g., state ABA organizations). By working together, evidence-based practitioners can discuss what research has been conducted since the last credible review was conducted and the limitations of the data that have been published (e.g., accurate picture of the participants and how similar they are to your clients). In addition, if local professional organizations play this role, they can help evidence-based practitioners to identify barriers that may need to be overcome in different settings. For example, a practitioner consulting in schools could clarify challenges they face in treatment implementation and then brainstorm with practitioners working in centers or home-based settings. By moving past the brainstorming phase and discussing strategies for realistically and meaningfully addressing these barriers, all members of the local organization can become better evidence-based practitioners.

Evidence-based practitioners can also support one another in acknowledging that it is reasonable to reject a treatment that has strong empirical support due to target, stakeholder, and client concerns. When evidence-based practitioners support each other in developing skills for effective collaboration and professional relationship management, they will better develop their professional judgment (Drisko & Grady, 2015). Evidence-based practitioners should be familiar with common barriers to implementing treatments such as:

- High start-up costs (Powers, Bowen, & Bowen; 2010) and insufficient resources (Cawood, 2010),
- Problems with training (Cawood, 2010; Powers et al., 2010),
- Accessing sufficient staffing (Cawood, 2010; Powers et al., 2010),
- Competing demands (Cawood, 2010),
- Time limitations (Cawood, 2010), and
- Insufficient administrative support (Cawood, 2010).

Evidence-based practitioners will need to problem-solve in order to determine the extent to which a treatment has a good contextual fit given the challenges these barriers may create. There are an untold number of variations in how effective autism treatments can be implemented, so evidence-based practitioners may need to be creative when assessing the likelihood an intervention could be a good match for the contextual environment. Detrich (1999) provides an example of how creative assessment can help select the right treatment. He assessed interactions in terms of the: (1) frequency of interactions between teachers and students, (2) the timing of their interactions, and (3) the relationship between the intervention practice and the student characteristics (e.g., examine those behaviors in the natural environment that are most likely to evoke reinforcement and then teach the target child a functionally equivalent behavior). Detrich (1999) called this a discrepancy analysis and when these variables all match the current supporting environment, a treatment is much more likely to be implemented with fidelity. In contrast, mismatches should send up red flags that treatment fidelity may be difficult to achieve. For example, when the staff tend to be more responsive to problem behavior than appropriate behavior, developing an intervention that is purely based on attending to appropriate behavior may lead to poor fidelity. If this type of intervention is suggested, higher levels of training and coaching may be needed, and this will require additional resources and environmental supports.

It would be much nicer to conclude this chapter with absolute rules evidence-based practitioners can apply to ensure that they always generate the right solution. Unfortunately, no such rules exist. Any attempt to create such rules would likely remove the critical role professional judgment plays in the EBP process. Although this process requires a great deal of effort on the part of the evidence-based practitioner, it is likely to result in client improvements because treatments that are effective, match the needs of the target client, are feasible, and have been shown to work for the target client are most likely to produce socially meaningful outcomes.

EXAMPLES

It should be clear that the EBP process should yield different outcomes for different clients with ASD. Many effective treatment options exist based on reviews of the literature. The appropriateness of those treatments are influenced by target, stakeholder, and client variables. Three illustrative examples are offered below to demonstrate how the EBP process can be applied with clients who begin with different practical questions and different characteristics, needs, and preferences. The outcomes described would vary with even minor changes in the target, stakeholder, and leader client variables—which is how the EBP process should be. It is also fine if, as an evidence-based practitioner, you would draw different conclusions. As long as evidence-based practitioners give serious consideration to all relevant sources of evidence and target, stakeholder, and client variables, they are using the EBP process the way it is intended to be used. In order to save space, only those variables that have direct bearing on the case example are described. However, evidence-based practitioners should assume that all relevant variables should be examined for each case.

Example 1: Charleze, a Six-Year-Old Girl With ASD
Practical question: Charleze flaps her hands and flicks her fingers so often that it interferes with her opportunities to interact with others and to meaningfully benefit from both her education and therapeutic services. Her parents, teachers, and therapists seek an intervention that will reduce this stereotypic behavior and increase how engaged she is in her activities.

Step 1. Multiple Sources of Evidence
Current client data, results of a systematic review, and client history offer significant evidence that helps prioritize treatment options.

Current Client Data
A functional analysis identified automatic reinforcement as the function of behavior.

Systematic Review
- Medication-based interventions for stereotypic behavior include Risperidone & aripiprazole (based on McPheeters et al., 2011).
- Based on the results of the National Standards Project 2.0 (NAC, 2015), the following treatments can be effective with stereotypic behaviors: behavioral interventions, parent training, peer training, self-management, and social skills package

Client History
- The parents reported that Risperidone had been attempted in the past and that it did not meaningfully reduce the hand-flapping and finger-flicking. Although minor reductions occurred, the parents did not feel this outweighed the side effects (e.g., sleep problems, weight gain, and extrapyramidal effects). They were not interested in considering other medication options.
- A preference assessment had been conducted previously and the items identified did not significantly reduce Charleze's hand-flapping or finger-flicking. Although minor reductions occurred, the family and teachers indicated that getting Charleze to pay attention during the preference assessment was time-consuming, and they did not trust the results they obtained.
- Social skills training has been attempted previously and Charleze's hand-flapping and finger-flicking actually increased. Although treatment fidelity data were strong, the school psychologist believed that Charleze could not be provided sufficient individualized attention when she attended sessions. When attention was delivered primarily to Charleze, the other children were extremely distractible. No one made progress.

Conclusions after reviewing evidence: Charleze's parents were encouraged to consider discussing medication options with their doctor and were reminded to seriously consider the potential side effects of medication for treating a behavior that is likely treatable via behavioral intervention. The parents found medication to be an undesirable option. Medication has been eliminated as an option at this time, unless the parents indicate their views have changed. The educational and behavioral treatment options were reviewed. Social skills training was given a lower priority because it resulted in an increase in stereotypic behaviors in the past. The capacity to deliver sufficient support to Charleze for peer training was also questionable because it required more staff effort and is dependent on peer compliance/performance. For this reason, peer training was deprioritized (i.e., given a lower priority) at this point. Treatments with a high priority include: behavioral interventions, parent training, and self-management. Alternative preference assessment procedures could prove useful, so basing a behavioral intervention around a preference assessment was only slightly deprioritized.

Step 2: Relevant Target Client Variables
Preference
Environmental enrichment is a treatment option that increases preference opportunities because it is only effective if the stimuli that are used are interesting or valuable to the target client. The literature shows that stimuli based on preference assessment may not produce the best possible outcomes for stereotypic behaviors, however. Competing items assessments evaluate the volume (frequency, intensity, and/or duration) of problem behavior that occur when in the presence of stimuli that are incompatible with the problem behavior. That is, stimuli that cannot occur at the same time as stereotypic behaviors are presented to the client and the level of stereotypic behavior is measured. Although items identified through a preference assessment often serve as reinforcers, they may still allow the stereotypic behavior to occur. Competing items assessments have produced better outcomes for reducing stereotypic behavior than preference assessment in some cases (Groskreutz, Groskreutz, & Higbee, 2011).

Client Repertoire
The family, teacher, and behavioral therapist question whether or not Charleze has the capacity to use a self-management strategy because she has no history of assessing her own behavior or seeking contingent reinforcement. She self-selects hand-flapping and finger-flicking.

Social Validity
Behavioral interventions in the form of environmental enrichment based on competing items assessments and self-management are most likely to increase generalization across environments because they can be used by parents, teachers, and therapists. Due to her challenges in communication, no treatment acceptability assessment tools were used with Charleze, but a plan to assess tolerability post-treatment implementation was planned.

Conclusions after reviewing target client variables: Environmental enrichment has been given a very high priority.

Step 3: Assess Stakeholder and Leader Variables
Relevant Stakeholder Variables
The family believes parent training would be an excellent choice. They are open to environmental enrichment but expressed concerns about whether or not Charleze could self-manage. Both the parents and the special education teacher indicated that they would need training to implement any of the treatments. The parents are particularly concerned about what to do when they are less available (e.g., making dinner, bathing, etc.). The special education teacher has used self-management previously with other clients and is uncertain how it could be used with Charleze.

Relevant Leader Variables
The principal and director of special education are open to environmental enrichment but have concerns about the cost of materials and the process of identifying materials that could be used for educational purposes. They leave the decision regarding self-management to the teacher.

Step 4: Identify short- and long-term goals
Conclusions after reviewing all relevant information: After discussing the evidence and all relevant target, stakeholder, and leader needs and concerns, an implementation plan was developed focusing on these treatment decisions:

- Short-term treatment—The schedule for all short- and long-term treatments were clearly outlined in an implementation plan.
  - The evidence-based practitioner will conduct competing items assessments at home and at school. The behavioral therapist working in the home can complete this assessment and incorporate environmental enrichment with limited training.

- The competing items assessment will be completed using stimuli already available at home and school. Identified stimuli will be available at home during times when adults are less available. They will be used at school in two ways: (1) educational materials that compete with the stereotypic behavior during structured educational periods and (2) play materials provided during less structured times.
- If a sufficient volume of stimuli are not identified with materials already available, a range of stimuli may need to be purchased or reallocated. Decisions about purchasing materials and material reallocation will be made based on discussion among stakeholder and leader clients.
- Training for environmental enrichment will occur for parents and Charleze's teacher. The teacher was previously trained in using naturalistic strategies and plans to use these techniques with the competing educational materials.
- Long-term treatment
  - A referral is made to the parents for a behavioral psychologist who can provide parent training. The parents will pursue this after the environmental enrichment strategy has been in place for at least 3–4 weeks, so they are not overwhelmed with information from different professionals.
  - Self-management does not seem viable at this time, but a plan to build Charleze's repertoire so it becomes practical in the future is developed. The parents and Charleze's teacher will begin scheduling reinforcement for engagement with peers, educational materials, and preferred toys and activities. A plan is outlined to move this system from a simple reinforcement system to a self-management system over the course of the next year.
  - Peer training will be attempted once Charleze is more consistently engaging with appropriate materials. In this way same-aged peers will be more willing to approach her and she does not have to be removed from the classroom for the social skills program. The teacher, school psychologist, and evidence-based practitioner have agreed to reconvene in 4 months or less to discuss this option further.

Step 5: Review New Evidence

- The parents, teacher, and behavior therapist all collect momentary time sampling data. However the behavior therapist collects momentary time sampling using a 10-second interval and the parents/teacher collect momentary time sampling data based on 15-minute intervals. These intervals were selected based on the competing demands faced by parents and teachers during environmental enrichment implementation.

- Because the treatment was being implemented across three settings, a multiple baseline design across settings was used to assess Charleze's progress.
- Although some materials needed to be purchased, Charleze significantly increased her appropriate engagement with materials across settings. Charleze used these materials enthusiastically and her affect has changed from flat to happy.
- Treatment fidelity data are good and there have been no problems with the quality of adherence. The implementation schedule was delayed slightly when the teacher was sick, but the delay was short.
- Stakeholder and leader clients are satisfied with the intervention. The resources required to perform the competing behavior assessment and environmental enrichment did not exceed the budget. Furthermore, those items that did not compete with Charleze's hand-flapping and finger-flicking have been used with other students in the school.
- After 6 weeks, parents began parent training. Her parents were extremely pleased that Charleze became more engaged with her parents after parent training was initiated.

Step 6: Determine Next Steps
- The evidence-based practitioner provided the teacher training/coaching for the peer training intervention after 2 months. The school psychologist attended training and is scheduling visits to the classroom to support these efforts. Peers have been trained but still require a lot of prompting from the teacher. They have been taught to initiate with other students during the training phase. After an additional 2 months, peer training will be initiated at school with Charleze as the target.
- Charleze's academic skills have improved subsequent to the implementation of environmental enrichment. Once she initiated and used educational materials, she began developing new academic skills that were listed on her Individualized Education Plan. Charleze's teacher is identifying new instructional materials that can be used in a competing behavior assessment to address new academic targets.

Example 2: Daniel, 17-Year-Old With ASD

Practical question: Daniel is involved in a school-to-work program that involves job shadowing. Daniel has learned to respond to social bids from others, but he is not initiating many interactions in this setting. "How can we increase his social initiations with the people he is job shadowing (e.g., asking questions, commenting about work)?"

Step 1: Multiple Sources of Evidence

Three sources of evidence are relevant: systematic review, client history, and current client data.

Systematic Review

The Evidence-Based Practices for Children, Youth, and Young Adults with Autism Spectrum Disorder Report (http://autismpdc.fpg.unc.edu/sites/autismpdc.fpg.unc.edu/files/imce/documents/2014-EBP-Report.pdf) identifies eight interventions that have been used to address communication skills in adolescents that are approximately Daniel's age. These are: antecedent-based intervention, extinction, functional communication training (FCT), modeling, reinforcement, scripting, technology aided instruction & intervention (TAII), and time delay.

Client History

Antecedent-based intervention, modeling, reinforcement-based interventions, and scripting with a time delay prompt have all been used successfully with Daniel in recent years, but this has been for other skills (e.g., acquisition of work skills, increasing attention to task).

Current Client Data

Deficits in social initiations have only occurred during the job shadowing component of the school-to-work program. Social initiations have been adequate in other settings. Observations of job shadowing suggest that social initiations are more frequent with the male than female employees he shadows.

Conclusions after reviewing evidence: All of the previously successful interventions that have been used for other skills should be given a priority. FCT and TAII should be deprioritized given Daniel's current communication skill set across other relevant environments. Extinction is inappropriate for the goal of increasing social initiations, so it should be eliminated.

Step 2: Relevant Client Variables
Health
Daniel reports that he is highly nervous in unstructured situations that are unfamiliar. Although he does not have a diagnosis of an anxiety disorder, he may require supports designed to help adolescents with ASD to self-manage under anxiety-provoking situations. He did not like the idea of using medication for this purpose and it would be preferable to use behavioral intervention as a frontline treatment for anxiety.

Repertoire
Daniel is able to initiate and respond to bids for social attention with others (e.g., teachers, parents, peers) in his everyday life.

Preference
Each of the treatment options is explained to Daniel. He preferred a treatment that does not make him stand out in the job setting. In fact, Daniel flushed and stopped initiating social interactions with the interviewer when the ideas of FCT, TAII, and modeling were described.

Social Validity
Daniel rated all treatments as acceptable except FCT, TAII, and modeling. Interventions that were more likely to help him use skills in unfamiliar situations (generalize) were reviewed. Daniel preferred scripting with a time delay prompt as long as the script could be reviewed before he went to the work site. This treatment was not ranked any higher than other options on the treatment acceptability scale.

Conclusions after reviewing target client variables: Daniel's preference seems to be scripting with time delay, as long as the script is read prior to being in the workplace. The combination of these treatments should be given a higher priority than other options; however, other options were not eliminated.

Step 3: Assess Stakeholder and Leader Variables
Relevant Stakeholder Variables
• The school is providing the treatment so the parents have no concerns about the costs, but they do not want to feel pressured to put Daniel on medication. When he was younger, they felt regularly pressured to put him on medication for his activity level, and they avoid medication usage in their household.

- Daniel's parents were initially concerned about Daniel seeing a therapist. When the discussion centered around skill development when facing anxiety-producing situations, they were more comfortable with this idea. The names of a few local cognitive behavioral therapists were given to them for this purpose. Cognitive behavioral interventions have research support for individuals with ASD (NAC, 2015).
- Daniel's views about FCT, TAII, and modeling were shared with his parents (with his permission). They agreed that these should be eliminated from the list of options.
- Daniel's parents reported that in their culture, younger individuals are expected to be deferential to older individuals. The remaining treatments were acceptable to them as long as he was taught to respectfully approach the employees serving as job models.
- If scripting was selected, the parents reported wanting to also have him read the script with them at home the morning before he job shadows employees.
- Daniel's teachers had no concerns about implementing the script with fidelity. For the time delay to be effective, job models (during job shadowing) would need to receive training. Because there are multiple sites Daniel could visit during the year, they requested that the training be as convenient as possible for job models. They were worried that job models may drop out of the program if the demand on them was too great.

Relevant Leader Variables
- Daniel's principal and special education director had no concerns with the treatments as long as they did not require additional resources.
- The school superintendent was friends with some of the executives at job sites where job shadowing occurred. He was concerned that it would place a demand on employers.

Step 4: Identify Long- and Short-Term Treatment Plans
Only one plan was developed.

- The treatment that was most preferred, was highly acceptable, and could be easily adapted to address the concerns of all parties was scripting with a time delay prompt.
- A short-training PSI (personalized system of instruction) was developed using PowerPoint so that all job models could complete

training independently and within a short period of time (antici-pated completion time: less than 10 minutes).
- The script was reviewed by Daniel's parents to ensure it was cultur-ally sensitive to their concerns.
- Daniel's parents elected to take him to a therapist for his anxiety in new situations.
- Daniel's parents were given a copy of the script after they completed the PSI.
- The treatment was implemented across settings.

Step 5: Review New Evidence
- Because there were limited opportunities to job shadow during the year, the only SSRD viable was an AB design. Daniel's social initia-tions increased with male job shadows after the treatment was implemented. He asked relevant questions and commented appro-priately about the workplace and the job.
- Daniel's social initiations did not increase significantly with female job models.
- Treatment fidelity data show that all job models used the time delay prompt at the job site. However, male job models had lower treat-ment fidelity because they waited silently for a longer period of time for Daniel to respond (even when they should have prompted sooner). The average delay before prompting was 10 seconds.
- The school superintendent did not hear complaints from employers.
- The teachers liked the PSI and reported that they would like to use it when training new paraprofessionals.

Step 6: Determine Next Steps
- Because the skill set was clearly within his repertoire, the treatment was modified so that female job models were taught to wait longer before prompting Daniel. This was the smallest adaptation from the current program and only required that female job models wait longer in silence.
- If this intervention was not successful, the team determined that a treatment package combining a Social Story that specifically tar-geted social initiations with females in the workplace with research-supported behavioral prompting and reinforcement procedures would be developed. The parents asked to review the Social Story before it was implemented to ensure that it was culturally sensitive.

Example 3: Stan, a 13-Year-Old With ASD

Practical question: Stan has been attending a summer autism camp for the past 4 years as a camper. This year he has graduated to become a "junior staff member." Although his job is to model appropriate behavior for beginning campers, he has begun yelling at the staff, crying, and disrupting camp activities. The camp would like him to retain his role as a junior staff member but they need him to model appropriate behavior. "How can they change his behavior?"

Step 1. Multiple Sources of Evidence

Current client data, results of a systematic review, and client history offer significant evidence that helps prioritize treatment options.

Current Client Data

Although a complete functional behavioral assessment was not completed, staff determined that Stan's disruptive behavior consistently happened *immediately* after they announced it was the end of an activity. The disruptive behaviors continued for approximately 5 minutes or until the next activity was initiated. The staff noted that this is the least structured part of the day and that it often took 5−7 minutes before the next activity was initiated.

Systematic Review
- Although systematic reviews have shown lithium and risperdone have effectively reduced disruptive behavior, the low frequency of the disruptive behavior outside the camp setting and the low risk associated with the behavior means that medication interventions are not appropriate.
- Based on the results of the National Standards Project 2.0 (NAC, 2015), the following treatments can be effective with problem behaviors for children Stan's age: behavioral interventions, cognitive behavioral interventions, modeling, parent training, social skills training, and story-based interventions.

Client History

When Stan entered middle school, he demonstrated similar disruptive behaviors immediately prior to the end of class. His teachers agreed to give him a 5-minute warning prior to the end of class plus Stan was given specific directions on what to do (e.g., write down what homework he needed to do and put his books and papers in a pile to be taken to his locker).

Conclusions after reviewing evidence: Parent training was deprioritized because he was not experiencing problems in the home. Social skills training was deprioritized because he already possessed the skills he needed, he merely needed to demonstrate those behaviors during the transition away from camp activities. Behavioral interventions in the form of antecedent interventions (i.e., the 5-minute warning + instructions) have been effective in the past and are not highly intrusive so this was given a high priority. Cognitive behavior interventions, social skills training, and modeling were retained as reasonable options.

Step 2: Relevant Target Client Variables
Social Validity–Treatment Acceptability
All treatment options were reviewed with Stan. He preferred the 5-minute warning + instructions. In fact, he said, "They should do this for all campers" and "I used to get upset as a camper when I didn't know what was coming next." He also reported that he was not sure what his role as a junior staff member was supposed to be during this time. He said he thought he was supposed to yell at staff because, "It is chaos at the end of activities and the staff members are all running around shouting orders to each other."

Client Repertoire
Stan already possesses all of the social skills needed as evidence by the fact he is serving as a good role model for campers at times other than the transition out of an activity.

Conclusions after reviewing target client variables: Social skills training was deprioritized because Stan already possesses the social skills needed. The antecedent intervention (i.e., the 5-minute warning + instructions) is highly acceptable and remains a high priority. In addition, modeling is prioritized because Stan is already copying the models provided by the staff. From his perspective, they shout orders at each other. If they model an appropriate tone of voice and a lessened sense of urgency at the end of tasks, his disruptive behaviors are likely to decrease.

Step 3: Assess Stakeholder and Leader Variables
Relevant Stakeholder Variables
His parents liked the idea of using the same strategy that was used at school. The camp staff agreed that they "probably do look like they are running around ordering each other what to do," from Stan's

perspective. Staff reported liking the idea of modeling more appropriate behavior for Stan.

Relevant Leader Variables
The camp director felt the 5-minute warning + instructions strategy was good for all of the campers and he liked that that Stan would not appear like he was being targeted for treatment. He agreed that his staff sometimes became anxious at the end of an activity due to time constraints and, as a result, sometimes modeled behavior that could be confused with yelling. Both strategies were not going to burden the camp financially or in terms of demands on staff. If effective, this treatment would allow Stan to remain in his role as "junior staff member."

Step 4: Identify Long- and Short-Term Treatment Plans
Conclusions after reviewing all relevant information: After discussing the evidence and all relevant target, stakeholder, and leader needs and concerns, an implementation plan was developed focusing on: (1) An antecedent intervention of giving Stan a 5-minute warning + instructions and (2) Modeling of appropriate staff tone and level of urgency during transition periods. Because it was a behavioral camp for ASD, the staff were prepared to implement the intervention immediately.

Step 5: Review New Evidence
The data showed a significant decrease in Stan's disruptive behavior during transition periods. However, a low but stable pattern of yelling at staff and crying continued. An examination of the treatment fidelity data showed poor implementation accuracy on the part of one staff member (Jancie). When interviewed, Jancie said, "I kind of like the melee at the end of the activity. I think that is what summer camp is about! Shouldn't we just let kids be kids?"

Step 6: Determine Next Steps
After reviewing the new evidence with the camp director, the current treatment was retained. However the camp director decided he wanted to give Stan a few choices (with his parents' permission). First, he could decide not to work with Jancie and could work with another camp staff member during that time. Second, he could continue to work with Jancie but he would need to use his own 5-minute warning system. Jancie and the other camp staff would develop some instructions he could generally use during this period. He would also have to

remind himself that he should not yell even when Jancie was yelling. Third, the director could try to get Jancie to use the system more effectively, but because it was only a 6-week camp, he did not think this was likely to work. Stan's parents agreed to buy him a watch with a "countdown" timer because Stan wanted to continue working with Jancie. He wanted to try using the 5-minute warning himself and thought it would be better if he did this at school too. All staff members were trained to prompt Stan to use the countdown timer at the beginning of activities so he would be warned when there were only 5 minutes left. Although rudimentary self-management systems like these have generally been shown to be effective with older children with ASD (NAC, 2015), but it also proved effective with Stan. The camp director reported that he was thrilled "not to have to try to change Jancie's behavior" this summer but shared that he did not plan to hire her again the next year. She had many strengths but he was concerned about her treatment fidelity based on her personal views. He feared this could impact the campers and thought it was important for all camp staff to model appropriate behavior. Although he respected her right to hold her views, he did not like that she seemed unconcerned about the possible impact on Stan. Specifically, her failure to implement the intervention could have meant that Stan's opportunities could have been restricted. Although Jancie did not come back to camp the next summer, Stan did. He was a junior staff member and used his self-management system entirely on his own!

Evidence-Based Practice Guide

ASK THE PRACTICAL QUESTION THAT IS RELEVANT IN THE CURRENT CASE. ARE THERE OTHER PRACTICAL QUESTIONS THAT SHOULD BE ASKED?

Steps	Weighing and Integrating Information

1. Identify best source(s) of evidence.
Evidence:
• Systematic reviews and meta-analysis
• Narrative review (consensus or critical)
• Practice guideline
• Principles
• Client history:
  • Confounding explanations
  • Treatment fidelity
  • Different environmental conditions
• Current client data
  • Functional behavior assessment
  • Other relevant data
• Notes (use this space to describe how these data are being weighed)
	A. "Is there evidence from a credible systematic review or meta-analysis that answers the practical question?"
	  i. If yes, list all effective treatments.
	  ii. "If no, is there evidence from consensus reviews, critical reviews, or practice guidelines?"
	B. "Are there treatments that do not seem consistent with scientific principles of behavior?"
	  i. If yes, consider giving these options a lower priority. Do not eliminate them from consideration at this point.
	  ii. If no, retain all options.
	C. "Is there credible evidence from the client's history that shows one of the remaining treatments will not work?"
	  i. If yes, confirm treatment fidelity data showed the intervention was implemented accurately.
	  ii. If no, retain all options.
	D. "Are there data that have been (or should be) collected to help identify the most effective treatment?"
	  i. If yes, identify remaining treatments that best match current data and prioritize those.
	  ii. If no, consider collecting these data (if possible).
	E. Construct list of "best" treatments based on A–E
	F. Construct list of alternative interventions (i.e., lower priority from parts A–E and those that have emerging but weaker evidence).

2. Review relevant target client variables that could impact treatment selection. Target client:
• Health
  • Medication
  • Medical and comorbid conditions
  • Biological variables
  • Mental health
	A. "Are there health reasons to strengthen or weaken the likelihood a treatment should be selected?" Prioritize lists accordingly (i.e., treatments that match target client needs given higher priority than treatments that do not).
	B. Examine treatments in relation to client repertoire.

(Continued)

(Continued)	
Steps	**Weighing and Integrating Information**

• Repertoire
  • Prerequisite skills
  • Behavioral cusps
• Preference
  • Preference assessment
  • Choice
  • Preference as a natural by-product of treatment
• Social validity
  • Quality of life
  • Generalization
  • Treatment acceptability
• Notes (use this space to describe how these data are being weighed)
	i. If client does not have prerequisite skills, eliminate or lower priority[a] for intervention.
	ii. If treatment can result in behavioral cusp, give the treatment a higher priority.
	C. Assessment of target client preference.
	  i. If preference assessment completed, incorporate results into consequence-based interventions and give treatment a higher priority.
	  ii. If choice incorporated, give treatment a higher priority.
	  iii. If preference a natural by-product of the treatment being implemented, give the intervention a higher priority.
	D. Review the treatments for social validity. Give a higher priority to treatments that:
	  i. Improve quality of life.
	  ii. Increase the likelihood generalization will occur.
	  iii. Are acceptable to the target client.
	E. Review list to ensure all relevant target client variables have influenced priority of lists.
	
	[a]A treatment may be temporarily eliminated but a plan to build skill may be part of a long-term solution.

3. Review relevant stakeholder and leader client variables that could impact treatment selection.
Stakeholder client(s):
• Social validity
  • Family quality of life
  • Feasibility
    − Resource constraint
    − Environmental supports
      o Family engagement
      o Childcare
      o Expectations clarified
      o Match with cultural norms
      o Stakeholder attitudes
      o Experience
      o Characteristics of staff providing treatment
      o Flexibility of training
      o Realistic appraisal of barriers
      o Appropriate training for stakeholder clients
    − Treatment fidelity
    − Treatment acceptability
  • Sustainability
Leader client(s):
• Feasibility
  • Expected value
  • Staff experience
  • Treatment complexity
	A. Review treatments for social validity. Give a higher priority to treatments that improve family quality of life (particularly for children and adolescents).
	B. Review treatments for feasibility. Give a higher priority to treatments that:
	  a. Is within the cost range identified by stakeholder or leader clients. If it is not within cost range, can resources be reallocated? If yes, it may not need a lower priority.
	  b. Can be implemented with sufficient environmental supports. Consider the following factors:
	    i. "What are the previous experiences of staff?"
	    ii. "Is there a sufficient number of staff?"
	    iii. "Are there support personnel who can assist?"
	  c. Can be implemented with treatment fidelity (with or without additional training).
	  d. Have a positive impact on the organization.
	  e. Require a lower response effort for stakeholder and leader clients.
	  f. Matches cultural norms of the organization.
	  g. Is associated with positive "attitudes" by stakeholder and leader clients.
	  h. Can be adapted without sacrificing target client progress.

(Continued)

(Continued)	
Steps	**Weighing and Integrating Information**

• Organizational impact
• Secure new resources
• Resource reallocation
• New collaborative partnerships
• Leader response effort
• Staffing requirements
• Impact on clients
• Generalizable to other clients
• Match with cultural norms
• Leader and staff attitudes
• Adaptability
• Sustainability
• Notes (use this space to describe how these data are being weighed)
	C. Additional considerations:
	  a. Treatments that are likely to be used with other clients should be given higher priority.
	  b. Treatments that are very complex should be given lower priority unless progress is believed possible only with complex treatment.
	D. Review treatment for sustainability. Consider items 3B.

4. Identify short- and long-term goals	A. "Is there a treatment (or combination of treatments) that can answer the practical question that started this process?" B. "If more than one treatment is selected, should they be introduced sequentially or simultaneously?," "Has the issue of treatment fidelity/feasibility and complex interventions been addressed with stakeholder and leader clients?" C. "Are there treatments that would best support the client but are not feasible?," "Should there be a plan to build capacity to implement this intervention?"
IMPLEMENT AND REVIEW TREATMENT **Ask question about implementation planning**	

5. **Review new evidence Evidence:**
• Target behavior progress monitoring (target client)
  • Correct data collection method
    − Data collection system
    − Frequency of data collection
    − Credibility of data
    − Other data collection issues
  • Single subject research design
    − Picking the right SSRD
    − Explaining SSRD to Others
• Additional source of data
  • Treatment fidelity
  • Quality of adherence
  • Implementation as planned
  • Target client preference & tolerability
  • Target client satisfaction
  • Stakeholder client satisfaction
  • Leader client satisfaction
  • Using consumer satisfaction data
• Notes (use this space to describe how these data are being weighed)
	A. "Are (i.e., an ascending trend line for behavior/ skills to be increased or a descending trend for behaviors/skills to be decreased)?"
	  a. If yes, continue the treatment if there are no other contraindications (e.g., problems with tolerability or satisfaction).
	  b. If no, identify:
	    • "Is treatment fidelity low?" Retraining or additional coaching/performance feedback may be necessary.
	    • "Have reinforcers been accurately identified and are they being delivered on a rich enough schedule?" Alterations in reinforcers and schedule of reinforcement may be needed.
	    • "Are client history and current client data accurate (e.g., was the correct function of behavior identified)?" Additional data collection may be necessary.
	B. "Is a single-subject research design that clearly demonstrates treatment effectiveness being used?"
	  a. "If no, will stakeholder clients consider using a single-subject research design?"

(Continued)	
Steps	**Weighing and Integrating Information**
	C. "Is there evidence of treatment fidelity?" 　a. "If yes, can this be sustained?" 　b. If no, identify: 　　i. "Are there sufficient resources and environmental supports?" 　　ii. "Does the training used match the training model needed?" 　　iii. "Is the treatment feasible?" D. "Is the quality of adherence sufficient?" 　a. "If yes, can this be sustained?" 　b. If no, identify: 　　i. "Are there sufficient resources and environmental supports?" 　　ii. "Does the training used match the training model needed?" 　　iii. "Is the treatment feasible?" E. "Was the intervention implemented as planned?" 　a. "If yes, can this be sustained?" 　b. If no, identify: 　　i. "Are there sufficient resources and environmental supports?" 　　ii. "Does the training used match the training model needed?" 　　iii. "Is the treatment feasible?" F. "Is the target client reporting a preference for the treatment or suggesting it is intolerable in some way?" 　• If yes, consider treatment adaptation. Go to Step 6B. G. "Is the target client reporting a high level of consumer satisfaction?" 　• If no, consider treatment adaptation. Go to Step 6B. H. "Are the stakeholder clients reporting a high level of consumer satisfaction?" 　• If no, consider treatment adaptation. Go to Step 6B. I. "Is the leader client reporting a high level of consumer satisfaction?" 　• If no, consider treatment adaptation. Go to Step 6B.
6. **Determine next steps** • Notes (use this space to describe how these data are being weighed)	A. "Should the treatment be retained?" 　i. If yes, return to Step 4 for ongoing assessment. A plan for fading the treatment should be developed. 　ii. If no, proceed to Step 5B. B. "Does the treatment need to be adapted?" 　i. If yes: 　　• "What is the smallest adaptation possible to address area of challenge based on Step 4?" 　　• "Will the adaptations violate the principles upon which the treatment is based?"

(*Continued*)

(Continued)	
Steps	**Weighing and Integrating Information**
	• "Can the adaptation still result in client progress?" Return to Step 4 for ongoing assessment.
	ii. "Do answers to Step 5 suggest the treatment should not be adapted?"
	• If yes, reject treatment and return to Step 1.
	• No, return to Step 4 for ongoing assessment
	C. "Should the treatment be rejected?"
	i. If yes, return to Step 1.
	ii. If no, consider retaining or adapting the treatment.

Sample Implementation Plan Checklist

Note: This checklist is designed to prompt discussion about how to fully develop a plan that will lead to implementation with a client or a number of clients within an organization. Write dates that all relevant parties agree should be met next to each task. When more than one meeting is necessary, specify the meeting schedule. Identify obstacles and plans to overcome these barriers in the second column. Lastly, write the date a task was completed when all aspects of this section have been resolved completely. Note: Additional categories may be needed for some clients.

Plan Type (Short-Term; Long-Term)	Date Proposed	Key People Responsible	Coping Plan	Date Completed
Treatment description (attach additional page if needed)				
I. Materials/Resources • Materials needed • Funding source for materials • When will/are materials secured				
II. Training • Funding for training secured • Trainers identified/training approach described • Identify all people to be trained • Describe knowledge, experience, or relevant variables that should influence training • Schedule didactic instruction or personalized system of instruction • Ongoing feedback and coaching schedule (schedule)				

III. Data collection
• Develop data collections system for:
  • Target client progress
  • Treatment fidelity
  • Quality of adherence plan
  • Preference
  • Tolerability
  • Feasibility
  • Satisfaction data collection
• Establish single-subject research design to be used				

(Continued)

(Continued)

Plan Type (Short-Term; Long-Term)	Date Proposed	Key People Responsible	Coping Plan	Date Completed
III. Treatment Implementation • Identify unanticipated resource constraints • Identify unanticipated limitations to environmental supports				
IV. Analysis of Treatment Effectiveness • Review target client progress (schedule) • Review target client preference/tolerability (schedule) • Review stakeholder/leader satisfaction (schedule)				
V. Next steps • Date for fading treatment • Date for adaptation decisions (new implementation plan to be developed) • Rejection of existing treatment (new implementation plan to be developed)				

REFERENCES

Aarons, G. A., Somerfeld, D. H., Hecht, D. B., Silovsky, J. F., & Chaffin, M. J. (2009). The impact of evidence-based practice implementation and fidelity monitoring on staff turnover: Evidence for a protective effect. *Journal of Consulting and Clinical Psychology, 77*(2), 270–280.

Albin, R. W., Lucyshyn, J. M., Horner, R. H., & Flannery, K. B. (1996). Contextual fit for behavior support plans: A model for "goodness of fit." *Positive Behavioral Support: Including People with Difficult Behavior in the Community, 8,* 98.

Allen, K. D., & Warzak, W. J. (2000). The problem of parental nonadherence in clinical behavior analysis: Effective treatment is not enough. *Journal of Applied Behavior Analysis, 33,* 373–391.

Aparicio, L. V. M., Guarienti, F., Razza, L. B., Carvalho, A. F., Fregni, F., & Brunoni, A. R. (2016). A systematic review on the acceptability and tolerability of transcranial direct current stimulation treatment in neuropsychiatry trials. *Brain Stimulation, 9*(5), 671–681.

Arnold, L. E., Vitiello, B., McDougle, C., Scahill, L., Shah, B., Gonzalex, N. M., ... Tierney, E. (2003). Parent-defined target symptoms respond to risperidone in RUPP autism study: Customer approach to clinical trials. *Journal of the American Academy of Child & Adolescent Psychiatry, 42* (12), 1443–1450.

Backer, T. E., David, S. L., & Soucy, G. (1995). Reviewing the behavioral science knowledge base on technology transfer *(NIDA Research Monograph 155, NIH Publication No. 95-4035).* Rockville, MD: National Institute on Drug Abuse.

Bados, A., Balaguer, G., & Saldana, C. (2007). The efficacy of cognitive-behavioral therapy and the problem of drop-out. *Journal of Clinical Psychology, 63*(6), 585–592.

Behavior Analyst Certification Board (BACB). (2014). Behavior Analyst Certification Board professional and ethical compliance code for behavior analysts. Retrieved from http://bacb.com/wp-content/uploads/2015/08/150824-compliance-code-english.pdf.

Bellg, A., Borelli, B., Resnick, B., Hecht, J., Minicucci, D. S., Ory, M., & Czajkowski, S. (2004). Enhancing treatment fidelity in health behavior change studies: Best practices and recommendations from the NIH Behavior Change Consortium. *Health Psychology, 23*(5), 443–451.

Billingsley, B. S. (2004). Special teacher retention and attrition: A critical analysis of the research literature. *The Journal of Special Education, 38,* 39–55.

Boe, E. E., Bobbitt, S. A., & Cook, L. H. (1997). Whither didst thou go? Retention, reassignment, migration, and attribution of special and general education teachers from a national perspective. *The Journal of Special Education, 30*(4), 371–389.

Boehm, T. L., Carter, E. W., & Taylor, J. L. (2015). Family quality of life during the transition to adulthood for individuals with intellectual disability and/or autism spectrum disorder. *American Journal on Intellectual and Developmental Disabilities, 120*(5), 395–411.

Borelli, B., Sepinwall, D., Bellg, A. J., Breger, R., DeFrancesco, C., Sharp, D. L., ... Orwig, D. (2005). A new tool to assess treatment fidelity and evaluation of treatment fidelity across 10 years of health behavior research. *Journal of Consulting and Clinical Psychology, 73,* 852–860.

Bowen, D. J., Kreuter, M., Spring, B., Cofta-Woerpel, L., Linnan, L., Weiner, D., ... Fernandez, M. (2009). How we design feasibility studies. *American Journal of Preventative Medicine, 36*(5), 452–457.

Breau, L. M., McGrath, P. J., Camfield, C. S., & Finley, G. A. (2002). Psychometric properties of the non-communicating children's pain checklist-revised. *Pain, 99,* 349–357.

Brigham, T. A., & Sherman, J. A. (1973). Effects of choice and immediacy of reinforcement on single response and switching behavior of children. *Journal of the Experimental Analysis of Behavior, 19,* 425–435.

Brodhead, M. (2015). Maintaining professional relationships in an interdisciplinary setting: Strategies for navigating nonbehavioral treatment recommendations for individuals with autism. *Behavior Analysis in Practice, 8,* 70–78.

Buckley, T. W., Ente, A. P., & Ruef, M. B. (2014). Improving a family's overall quality of life through parent training in Pivotal Response Treatment. *Journal of Positive Behavior Interventions, 16*(1), 60–63.

Cawood, N. D. (2010). Barriers to the use of evidence-supported programs to address school violence. *Children & Schools, 32*(3), 143–149.

Cherniss, C. (1995). *Beyond Burnout: Helping teachers, nurses, therapists, and lawyers recover from stress and disillusionment.* New York, NY: Routledge.

Chorpita, B. F., & Nakamura, B. J. (2004). Four considerations for dissemination of intervention innovations. *Clinical Psychology: Scientific and Practice, 11,* 364–367.

Collier-Meek, M. A., Sanetti, L. M. H., & Boyle, A. M. (2015). Providing feasible implementation support: Direct training and implementation planning in consultation. *School Psychology Forum: Research in Practice, 10*(1), 106–119.

Council for Children with Behavioral Disorders. (2009). The use of physical restraint procedures in schools. Retrieved from http://www.casecec.org/pdf/seclusion/Accepted,%20CCBD%20on%20Use%20of%20Restraint,%207-8-09.pdf.

Courtemanche, A. B., Black, W. R., & Reese, R. M. (2016). The relationship between pain, self-injury, and other problem behaviors in young children with autism and other developmental disabilities. *American Journal on Intellectual and Developmental Disabilities, 121*(3), 194–203.

Cowan, R. J., & Allen, K. D. (2007). Using naturalistic procedures to enhance learning in individuals with autism: A focus on generalized teaching within school setting. *Psychology in the Schools, 44*(7), 701–715.

Dababnah, S., & Parish, S. L. (2016). Feasibility of an empirically based program for parents of preschoolers with autism spectrum disorder. *Autism, 20*(1), 85–95.

Dahl, N., Tervo, R., & Symons, F. J. (2007). Treatment acceptability of healthcare services for children with cerebral palsy. *Journal of Applied Research in Intellectual Disabilities, 20*(5), 475–482.

De Bruin, E. I., Ferdinand, R. F., Meester, S., deNijs, P. F. A., & Verheih, F. (2007). High rates of psychiatric comorbidity in PDD-NOS. *Journal of Autism and Developmental Disorders, 37,* 877–886.

Detrich, R. (1999). Increasing treatment fidelity by matching interventions to contextual variables within the educational setting. *School Psychology Review, 28*(4), 608–620.

Drisko, J. W., & Grady, M. D. (2015). Evidence-based practice in social work: A contemporary perspective. *Clinical Social Work Journal, 43,* 274–282.

Dufrene, B. A., Lestremau, L., & Zoder-Martell, K. (2014). Direct behavioral consultation: Effects on teachers' praise and student disruptive behavior. *Psychology in the Schools, 51*(6), 567–580.

Elliott, S. N. (1988). Acceptability of behavioral treatments: Review of variables that influence treatment selection. *Professional Psychology: Research and Practice, 19*(1), 68–80.

Elliott, S. N., Turco, T.L., Evans, S., & Gresham, F.M. (1984). Group contingency interventions: Children's acceptability ratings. In *Paper presented at the Meeting of the Association for the Advancement of Behavior Therapy,* Philadelphia, PA.

Elliott, S. N., & Von Brock Treuting, M. (1991). The Behavior Intervention Rating Scale: Development and validation of a pretreatment acceptability and effectiveness measure. *Journal of School Psychology, 29,* 43–51.

Elliott, S. N., Witt, J. C., Galvin, G. A., & Peterson, R. (1984). Acceptability of positive and reductive behavioral interventions: Factors that influence teachers' decisions. *Journal of School Psychology, 22*, 353–360.

Fisher, W. W., Thompson, R. H., Piazza, C. C., Crosland, K., & Gotjen, D. (1997). On the relative reinforcing effects of choice and differential consequences. *Journal of Applied Behavior Analysis, 30*(3), 423–438.

Fixsen, D. L., Blasé, K. A., Naoom, S. F., & Wallace, F. (2009). Core implementation components. *Research on Social Work Practice, 19*(5), 531–540.

Fore, C., Martin, C., & Bender, W. N. (2002). Teacher burnout in special education: The causes and the recommended solutions. *The High School Journal, 86*(1), 36–44.

Futernick, K. (2007). *A possible dream: Retaining California teachers so all students learn.* Sacramento, CA: California State University Center for Teacher Quality.

Gambrill, E. (2001). Social work: An authority-based profession. *Research on Social Work Practice, 11*(2), 166–175.

Garcia, G., Logan, G. E., & Gonzalez-Heydrich, J. (2012). Management of psychotropic side effects in children and adolescents. *Child and Adolescent Psychiatric Clinics of North America, 21*(4), 713–738.

Gedye, A. (1989). Extreme self-injury attributed to frontal lobe seizures. *American Journal on Mental Retardation, 94*(1), 20–26.

Gersten, R., Vaughn, S., Deshler, D., & Schiller, E. (1997). What we know about using research findings: Implications for improving special education. *Journal of Learning Disabilities, 30*(5), 466–476.

Gianoumis, S., Seiverling, L., & Sturmey, P. (2012). The effects of behavior skills training on correct teacher implementation of natural language paradigm teaching skills and child behavior. *Behavioral Interventions, 27*, 57–74.

Good, C. B., & Gelled, W. F. (2016). Off-label drug use and adverse drug events: Turning up the heat on off-label prescribing. *JAMA Internal Medicine, 176*(1), 63–64.

Gresham, F. M., MacMillan, D. L., Beebe-Frankenberger, M. E., & Bocian, K. M. (2000). Treatment integrity in learning disabilities intervention research: Do we really know how treatments are implemented? *Learning Disabilities Research & Practice, 15*(4), 198–205.

Groskreutz, M. P., Groskreutz, N. C., & Higbee, T. S. (2011). Response competition and stimulus preference in the treatment of automatically reinforced behavior: A comparison. *Journal of Applied Behavior Analysis, 44*(1), 211–215.

Hammond, R. K., & Hoffman, J. M. (2014). Adolescents with high-functioning autism: An investigation of comorbid anxiety and depression. *Journal of Mental Health Research in Intellecutal Disabilities, 7*(3), 246–263.

Hendricks, D. (2011). Special education teachers serving students with autism: A descriptive study of the characteristics and self-reported knowledge and practices employed. *Journal of Vocational Rehabilitation, 35*, 37–50.

Hennessey, M. L., & Rumrill, P. D., Jr (2003). Treatment fidelity in rehabilitation research. *Journal of Vocational Rehabilitation, 19*(3), 123–126.

Horner, R. H., Carr, E. G., Halle, J., McGee, G., Odom, S., & Wolery, M. (2005). The use of single-subject research to identify evidence-based practice in special education. *Exceptional Children, 71*(2), 165–179.

Ishida, T., Katagriri, T., Uchida, H., Takeuchi, H., Sakurai, H., Watanabe, K., & Mimura, M. (2014). Incidence of deep vein thrombosis in restrained patients. *Psychosomatics: Journal of Consultation and Liaison Psychiatry, 55*(1), 69–75.

Jennett, H. K., Harris, S. L., & Mesibov, G. B. (2003). Commitment to philosophy, teacher efficacy, and burnout among teachers of children with autism. *Journal of Autism and Developmental Disorders, 33*(6), 583−593.

Karst, J. S., & Van Hecke, A. V. (2012). Parent and family impact of autism spectrum disorders: A review and proposed model for intervention evaluation. *Clinical Child and Family Psychology Review, 15*(3), 247−277.

Kaufman, D., Codding, R. S., Markus, K. A., & Nagler, K. E. (2013). Effects of verbal and written performance feedback on treatment adherence: Practical application of two delivery formats. *Journal of Educational and Psychological Consultation, 23*(4), 264−299.

Kazdin, A. E. (1980). Acceptability of alternative treatments for deviant child behavior. *Journal of Applied Behavior Analysis, 132*, 259−273.

Kazdin, A. E. (2011). *Single-case research designs: Methods for clinical and applied settings* (2nd ed.). New York, NY: Oxford University Press.

Kazdin, A. E., French, N. H., & Sherick, R. B. (1981). Acceptability of alternative treatments for children: Evaluations by inpatient children, parents, and staff. *Journal of Consulting and Clinical Psychology, 49*, 900−907.

Kelley, M., Heffer, R., Gresham, F., & Elliott, S. (1989). Development of a modified treatment evaluation inventory. *Journal of Psychopathology and Behavioral Assessment, 11*, 235−247.

Kennedy, C. H., & Meyer, K. A. (1996). Sleep deprivation, allergy symptoms, and negatively reinforced behavior. *Journal of Applied Behavior Analysis, 29*(1), 133−135.

Khan, K. S., Kunz, R., Kleijnan, J., & Antes, G. (2003). Five steps to conducting a systematic review. *Journal of the Royal Society of Medicine, 96*, 118−121.

Koegel, L. K., Park, M. N., & Koegel, R. L. (2014). Using self-management to improve the reciprocal social conversation of children with autism spectrum disorder. *Journal of Autism and Developmental Disorders, 44*, 1055−1063.

Koegel, R. L., Bimbela, A., & Schreibman, L. (1996). Collateral effects of parent training on family interactions. *Journal of Autism and Developmental Disorders, 26*(3), 347−359.

Koegel, R. L., & Egel, A. L. (1979). Motivating autistic children. *Journal of Abnormal Psychology, 88*, 418−426.

Koegel, R. L., Egel, A. L., & Williams, J. A. (1980). Behavioral contrast and generalization across settings in the treatment of autistic children. *Journal of Experimental Child Psychology, 30*, 422−437.

Koegel, R. L., & Frea, W. D. (1993). Treatment of social behavior in autism through the modification of pivotal social skills. *Journal of Applied Behavior Analysis, 26*, 369−377.

Koegel, R. L., Werner, G. A., Vismara, L. A., & Koegel, L. K. (2005). The effectiveness of contextually supported play date interactions between children with autism and typically developing peers. *Research & Practice for Persons with Severe Disabilities, 30*(2), 93−102.

Koenig, K., White, S. W., Pachler, M., Lau, M., Lewis, M., Klin, A., & Scahill, L. (2010). Promoting social skill development in children with pervasive developmental disorders: A feasibility and efficacy study. *Journal of Autism and Developmental Disorders, 40*, 1209−1218.

Kolko, D. J., Hoagwood, K. E., & Springgate, B. (2010). Treatment research for children and youth exposed to traumatic events: Moving beyond efficacy to amp up public health impact. *General Hospital Psychiatry, 32*, 465−476.

Kronenberg, L., Slager-Visscher, K., Goossens, P., van Den Brink, W., & van Achterberg, T. (2014). Everyday life consequences of substance use in adult patients with a substance use disorder (SUD) and co-occurring attention deficit/hyperactivity disorder (ADHD) or autism spectrum disorder (ASD): A patient's perspective. *BMC Psychiatry, 14*, 264−279.

Kronenberg, L. M., Goossens, P. J. J., van Busschback, J., van Achterberg, T., & van den Brink, W. (2015). Coping styles in substance use disorder (SUD) patients with and without co-occurring attention deficit/hyperactivity disorder (ADHD) or autism spectrum disorder (ASD). *BMC Psychiatry*, *15*(1), 159−166.

Layer, S. A., Hanley, G. P., Heal, N. A., & Tiger, J. H. (2008). Determining individual preschoolers' preference in a group arrangement. *Journal of Applied Behavior Analysis*, *41*, 25−37.

Leucht, S., Kissling, W., & Davis, J. M. (2009). How to read and understand and use systematic reviews and meta-analyses. *Acta Psychiatry Scandanavia*, *119*, 443−450.

Liu, Y., Ni, H., Wang, C., Li, L., Cheng, Z., & Weng, Z. (2016). Effectiveness and tolerability of aripiprazole in children and adolescents with Tourette's disorder: A meta-analysis. *Journal of Child and Adolescent Psychopharmacology*, *26*(5), 436−441.

Lopata, C., Thomeer, M. L., Lipinski, A. M., Donnelly, J. P., Nelson, A. T., Smith, R. A., ... Volker, M. A. (2015). RCT examining the effect of treatment integrity for a psychosocial treatment for high-functioning children with ASD. *Research in Autism Spectrum Disorders*, *17*, 52−63.

Lopata, C., Toomey, J. A., Thomeer, M. L., McDonald, C. A., Fox, J. D., Smioth, R. A., ... Lipinski, A. M. (2015). Community trial of a comprehensive psychosocial treatment for HFASDs. *Focus on Autism and Other Developmental Disabilities*, *30*(2), 115−125.

Martens, B. K., Witt, J. C., Elliott, S. N., & Darveaux, D. X. (1985). Teacher judgments concerning the acceptability of school-based interventions. *Professional Psychology: Research and Practice*, *16*, 191−198.

Mautone, J. A., DuPaul, G. J., Jitendra, A. K., Tresco, K. E., Junod, R. V., & Volpe, R. J. (2009). The relationship between treatment integrity and acceptability of reading interventions for children with attention-deficit/hyperactivity disorder. *Psychology in the Schools*, *46*(10), 919−931.

McConnell, S. R., McEvoy, M. A., & Odom, S. L. (1992). Implementation of social competence interventions in early childhood special education classes: Current practices and future directions. In S. L. Odom, S. R. McConnell, & M. A. McEvoy (Eds.), *Social competence of young children with disabilities: Issues and strategies for intervention* (pp. 112−133). Baltimore, MD: Brookes.

McHugh, R. K., & Barlow, D. H. (2012). Dissemination and implementation of evidence-based psychological interventions: Current status and future directions. In R. K. McHugh, & D. H. Barlow (Eds.), *Dissemination and implementation of evidence-based psychological interventions* (pp. 247−264). New York, NY: Oxford University Press.

McKenney, E. L., & Brisol, R. M. (2014). Supporting intensive interventions for students with autism spectrum disorder: Performance feedback and discrete trial training. *School Psychology Quarterly*, *30*(1), 8−22.

McPheeters, M. L., Warren, Z., Sathe, N., Buzek, J. L., Krishaswami, S., Jerome, R. N., & Veenstra-VanderWeele, J. (2011). A systematic review of medical treatments for children with autism spectrum disorders. *Pediatrics*, *127*(5), 1312−1321.

Miller, D. L., & Kelley, M. L. (1992). Treatment acceptability: The effects of parent gender, marital adjustment, and child behavior. *Child & Family Behavior Therapy*, *14*(1), 11−23.

Moeller, J. D., Dattilo, J., & Rusch, F. (2015). Applying quality indicators to single-case research designs used in special education: A systematic review. *Psychology in the Schools*, *52*(2), 139−153.

Moher, D., Liberati, A., Tetzlaff, J., Altman, D. G., & The PRISMA Group (2009). Preferred reporting items for systematic reviews and meta-analyses: The PRISMA Statement. *Annals of Internal Medicine*, *151*(4), 264−269.

Morrier, M. J., Hess, K. L., & Heflin, L. J. (2011). Teacher training for implementation of teaching strategies for students with autism spectrum disorders. *Teacher Education and Special Education*, *34*(2), 119−132.

Musser, E. D., Hawkey, E., Kachan-Liu, S. S., Lees, P., Roullet, J. B., Goddard, K., & Igg, J. T. (2014). Shared familial transmission of autism spectrum and attention-deficit hyperactivity disorders. *Journal of Child Psychology and Psychiatry*, *55*, 819−827.

National Autism Center (2015). *Findings and conclusions: National standards project, phase 2*. Randolph, MA: National Autism Center.

Noell, G. H., Gansle, K. A., Mevers, J. L., Knox, R. M., Mintz, J. C., & Dahir, A. (2014). Improving treatment plan implementation in schools: A meta-analysis of single subject design studies. *Journal of Behavioral Education, 23*, 168–191.

Oono, I. P., Honey, E. J., & McConachie, H. (2013). Parent mediated early intervention for young children with autism spectrum disorders (ASD). *Evidence Based Child Health: A Cochrane Review Journal, 8*(6), 2380–2479.

Pahnke, J., Lundgren, T., Hursti, T., & Hirvikoski, T. (2013). Outcomes of acceptance and commitment therapy-based skills training group for students with high-functioning autism spectrum disorders: A quasi-experimental pilot study. *Autism, 18*(8), 1–12.

Pemberton, J. R., & Borrego, J., Jr (2005). The relationship between treatment acceptability and familism. *International Journal of Behavioral Consultation and Therapy, 1*(4), 329–337.

Pence, S. T., St. Peter, C. C., & Tetreault, A. S. (2012). Increasing accurate preference assessment implementation through pyramidal training. *Journal of Applied Behavior Analysis, 45*, 345–359.

Place, M. (2015). Do we need norms of fitness for children with autistic spectrum condition? *British Journal of Special Education, 42*(2), 199–216.

Power, T. J., Blom-Hoffman, J., Clarke, A. T., Riley-Tillman, T. C., Kelleer, C., & Manz, P. H. (2005). Reconceptualizing intervention integrity: A partnership-based framework for linking research with practice. *Psychology in the Schools, 42*(5), 495–507.

Powers, J. D., Bowen, N. K., & Bowen, G. L. (2010). Evidence-based programs in school settings: Barriers and recent advances. *Journal of Evidence-Based Social Work, 7*(4), 313–331.

Pugliese, C. E., & White, S. W. (2014). Brief report: Problem-solving therapy in college students with autism spectrum disorders: Feasibility and preliminary efficacy. *Journal of Autism and Developmental Disorders, 44*, 719–729.

Reimers, T. M., & Wacker, D. P. (1988). Parents' rating of the acceptability of behavioral treatment recommendation made in an outpatient clinic: A preliminary analysis of the influence of treatment effectiveness. *Behavioral Disorders, 14*, 7–15.

Reimers, T. M., Wacker, D. P., & Cooper, L. J. (1991). Evaluation of the acceptability of treatments for their children's behavioral difficulties: Ratings by parents receiving services in an outpatient clinic. *Child & Family Behavior Therapy, 13*(2), 53–71.

Reimers, T. M., Wacker, D. P., & Koeppl, G. (1987). Acceptability of behavioral interventions: A review of the literature. *School Psychology Review, 16*, 212–227.

Rogers, E. M. (2003). *Diffusion of innovations* (5th ed.). New York, NY: Free Press.

Rosales-Ruiz, J., & Baer, D. M. (1997). Behavioral cusps: A developmental and pragmatic concept for behavior analysis. *Journal of Applied Behavior Analysis, 30*, 533–544.

Rousseau, D. M. (1977). Technological differences in job characteristics, employee satisfaction, and motivation: A synthesis of job design research and sociotechnical systems theory. *Organizational Behavior and Human Performance, 19*, 18–42.

Rush, K. S., Moretenson, B. P., & Birch, S. E. (2010). Evaluation of preference assessment procedures for use with infants and toddlers. *International Journal, 6*(1), 2–16.

Russell, G., Rodgers, L. R., Ukoumunne, O. C., & Ford, T. (2014). Prevalence of parent-reported ASD and ADHD in the UK: Findings from the Millinnium Cohort Study. *Journal of Autism and Developmental Disorders, 44*, 31–40.

Sanetti, L. M. H., & Kratochwill, T. R. (2009). Toward developing a science of treatment integrity: Introduction to the special series. *School Psychology Review, 38*, 445–459.

Sanetti, L. M. H., Chafouleas, S. M., Fallon, L. M., & Jaffrey, R. (2014). Increasing teachers' adherence to a class-wide intervention through performance feedback provided by a school-based consultant: A case study. *Journal of Educational and Psychological Consultation, 24*(3), 239–260.

Sarver, N. W., Beidel, D. C., & Spitalnick, J. S. (2014). The feasibility and acceptability of virtual environments in the treatment of childhood social anxiety disorder. *Journal of Clinical Child and Adolescent Psychology, 43*(1), 63–73.

Schalock, R. L., Gardner, J. F., & Bradley, V. J. (2007). *Quality of life for people with intellectual and other developmental disabilities: Applications across individuals, organizations, communities, and systems.* Washington, DC: American Association on Intellectual and Developmental Disabilities.

Schoenwald, S. K., McHugh, R. K., & Barlow, D. H. (2012). The science of dissemination and implementation. In R. K. McHugh, & D. H. Barlow (Eds.), *Dissemination and implementation of evidence-based psychological interventions* (pp. 247–264). New York, NY: Oxford University Press.

Slocum, T. A., Detrich, R., & Spencer, T. D. (2012). Evaluating the validity of systematic reviews to identify empirically supported treatments. *Education and Treatment of Children, 35*(2), 201–233.

Slocum, T. A., Detrich, R., Wilczynski, S. M., Spencer, T. D., Lewis, T., & Wolfe, K. (2014). The evidence-based practice of applied behavior analysis. *The Behavior Analysts, 37*(1), 41–56.

Smith, S. W., Daunic, A. P., & Tayler, G. G. (2007). Treatment fidelity in applied educational research: Expanding the adoption and application of measures to ensure evidence-based practice. *Education and Treatment of Children, 30*(4), 121–134.

Spencer, T. D., Detrich, R., & Slocum, T. A. (2012). Evidence-based practice: A framework for making effective decisions. *Education and Treatment of Children, 35,* 127–151.

Spreat, S., & Walsh, D. E. (1994). Impact of treatment efficacy and professional affiliation on ratings of treatment acceptability. *Mental Retardation, 32*(3), 227–233.

Stahmer, A. C., Rieth, S., Lee, E., Resinger, E. M., Mandell, D. S., & Connell, J. E. (2015). Training teachers to use evidence-based practices for autism: Examining procedural implementation fidelity. *Psychology in the Schools, 52*(2), 181–195.

Standler, R.B. (2012, July 29). Legal right to refuse medical treatment in the USA. Retrieved from http://www.rbs2.com/rrmt.pdf.

Sterling-Turner, H. E., & Watson, T. S. (2002). An analog investigation of the relationship between treatment acceptability and treatment integrity. *Journal of Behavioral Education, 11*(1), 39–50.

Stokes, T. F., & Baer, D. M. (1977). An implicit technology of generalization. *Journal of Applied Behavior Analysis, 10,* 349–367.

Strain, P. S., Barton, E. E., & Dunlap, G. (2012). Lessons learned about the utility of social validity. *Education and Treatment of Children, 35*(2), 183–200.

Suhrheinrich, J., Stahmer, A. C., & Schreibman, L. (2007). A preliminary assessment of teachers' implementation of Pivotal Response Training. *The Journal of Speech-Language Pathology—Applied Behavior Analysis, 2*(1), 1–13.

Tarnowski, K. J., & Simonian, S. J. (1992). Assessing treatment acceptance: The abbreviated acceptability rating profile. *Journal of Behavior Therapy & Experimental Psychiatry, 23,* 101–106.

Tiger, J. H., Hanley, G. P., & Hernandez, E. (2006). An evaluation of the value of choice with preschool children. *Journal of Applied Behavior Analysis, 39*(1), 1–16.

Toussaint, K. A., Kodak, T., & Vladescu, J. C. (2016). An evaluation of choice on instructional efficacy and individual preferences among children with autism. *Journal of Applied Behavior Analysis, 49,* 170–175.

Turner-Brown, L. M., Perry, T. D., Dichter, G. S., Bodfish, J. W., & Penn, D. L. (2008). Brief report: Feasibility for adults with high functioning autism. *Journal of Autism and Developmental Disorders, 38,* 1777–1784.

van Iterson, L., De Jong, P. F., & Zijlstra, B. J. H. (2015). Pediatric epilepsy and comorbid reading disorders, math disorders, or autism spectrum disorders: Impact of epilepsy on cognitive patterns. *Epilepsy & Behavior, 44,* 159–168.

Vernon, T. W., Koegel, R. L., Dauterman, H., & Stolen, K. (2012). An early social engagement intervention for young children with autism and their parents. *Journal of Autism and Developmental Disorders, 42*(12), 2702–2717.

Virues-Ortega, J., Pritchard, K., Grant, R. L., North, S., Hurtado-Parrado, C., Lee, M. S. H., & Yu, C. T. (2014). Clinical decision making and preference assessment for individuals with intellectual disabilities. *American Journal of Intellectual and Developmental Disabilities, 119*(2), 151–170.

Vivanti, G., Paynter, J., Duncan, E., Fothergill, H., Dissanayake, C., Rogers, S. J., & the Victorian ASELCC Team (2014). Effectiveness and feasibility of the Early Start Denver Model implemented in a group-based community childcare setting. *Journal of Autism Developmental Disorders, 44,* 3140–3153.

Wacker, D. P., Steege, M. W., Northup, J., Sasso, G., Berg, W., Reimers, T., & Donn, L. (1990). A component analysis of functional communication training across three topographies of severe behavior problems. *Journal of Applied Behavior Analysis, 23,* 417–429.

Waller, G. (2009). Evidence-based treatment and therapist drift. *Behaviour Research and Therapy, 47,* 119–127.

Waller, G., & Turner, H. (2016). Therapist drift redux: Why well-meaning clinicians fail to deliver evidence-based therapy, and how to get back on track. *Behaviour Research and Therapy, 77,* 129–137.

Weisz, J. R., Jensen-Doss, A., & Hawley, K. M. (2006). Evidence-based youth psychotherapies versus usual clinical care: A meta-analysis of direct comparisons. *American Psychologist, 61*(7), 671–689.

White, S. W., Ollendick, T., Albano, A. M., Oswald, D., Johnson, C., Southam-Gerow, M. A., ... Scahill, L. (2013). Randomized controlled trial: Multimodal anxiety and social skill intervention for adolescents with autism spectrum disorder. *Journal of Autism and Developmental Disorders, 43,* 382–394.

Wilczynski, S. M. (2012). Risk and strategic decision-making in developing evidence-based practice guidelines. *Education and Treatment of Children, 35*(2), 291–311.

Wilczynski, S. M., Connolly, S., DuBard, M., Henderson, A., & McIntosh, D. (2015). Assessment, prevention, and intervention for abuse among individuals with disabilities. *Psychology in the Schools, 52*(1), 9–21.

Wilczynski, S.M., Henderson, A., Harris, N., Bostic, S.D., & Kosmala, S.D. (in press). Evidence-based practice, culture, and young children with Autism Spectrum Disorder. Perspectives on Early Childhood Psychology and Education, *1(2).*

Witt, J. C., & Elliott, S. N. (1985). Acceptability of classroom intervention strategies In T. Kratochwill (Ed.), *Advances in school psychology* (Vol. 4, pp. 251–288). Hillsdale, NJ: Erlbaum.

Witt, J. C., Moe, G., Gutkin, T. B., & Andrews, L. (1984). The effect of saying the same thing in different ways: The problem of language and jargon in school-based consultation. *Journal of School Psychology, 22*(4), 361–367.

Wolf, M. M. (1978). Social validity: The case for subjective measurement or how applied behavior analysis is finding its heart. *Journal of Applied Behavior Analysis, 11,* 203–214.

Wong, C., Odom, S. L., Hume, K. A., Cox, A. W., Fettig, A., Kucharczyk, S., ... Schultz, T. R. (2015). Evidence-based practices for children, youth, and young adults with autism spectrum disorder: A comprehensive review. *Journal of Autism and Developmental Disorders, 45*(7), 1951–1966.

INDEX

Note: Page numbers followed by "*t*" refer to tables.